The Otherness

A Personal Interaction

By

Tim Watts

authorHOUSE™

1663 LIBERTY DRIVE, SUITE 200
BLOOMINGTON, INDIANA 47403
(800) 839-8640
WWW.AUTHORHOUSE.COM

First published by AuthorHouse 11/08/04

ISBN: 1-4184-8868-2 (sc)

Printed in the United States of America
Bloomington, Indiana

This book is printed on acid-free paper.

If others see what I have seen
It must be a vision and not a dream

William Morris
Architect / Artist

First Published by

Sirius Publications

http://www.sirius-books.com

Acknowledgements

My most heartfelt gratitude will surprisingly be towards those who have no knowledge of this book or of my experiences. Close family and friends have proven to be the most solid without so much of an inkling of the double life I have led. As close as these people are, they will never experience either the brilliance or confusion that otherworldly interaction plunges you into and in so many ways I feel sad that I cannot share this insight.

I would also like to offer my condolences to those who have suffered at the hands of extraterrestrials or paranormal entities because my encounters have never been this way. I don't pretend to have the answers but consider the subject of interaction to be a science in itself offering a vastness of experience. There will certainly be a time brought about through a breakthrough when the subject of "high strangeness" will no longer be that way and the mystery behind personal experience will have been answered.

At the age of 34 there are endless questions in my life still unanswered but the relatively short history of strangeness I have led is deeply explored in these pages. I hope that the briefness of my story will perhaps herald a greater and more complete saga ahead like a seed waiting to hatch.

I will never stop waiting for the answer.

Table of Contents

Introduction

To an animal, the civilised world must appear a bizarre place. Their knee height perception of the things we do must appear as puzzling as it is awesome. Our purpose, our values, our use of time, cognition and memory are things we probably can't even translate within the animal kingdom. Reality must mean something quite different to different species.

Over the years, I have come to believe in the existence of another species, one that is not classified in our knowledge of the world. I am finally convinced of a higher kingdom of nature where reality is not only taken in through the five senses and our version of it is not necessarily the ultimate one.

I cannot help but compare the relationship we have with this higher world and its species to the relationship animals have with us. We have probably interacted unknowingly with other realms for centuries in ways we are not familiar with, ways in which our awareness and inquisitiveness stretches no further than that of a cage of gerbils when confronted with their "outside", the domain of their owners.

Having an awareness of the other side of nature is nothing new. People all through history have reported periods of high-strangeness, things which can only be labelled "unexplained". This is not unlike being the animal that curiously glimpses the comings and goings of our world and tries to register what it has seen. This other realm interacts with us at the strangest intervals and our ability to define it is sometimes as limited as the animal's. I sometimes wonder if our minds are deliberately designed not to solve the mystery of the universe or think beyond our reality any more than cattle are supposed to think beyond theirs.

I hope this is not so with the human race and that our evolution is limitless. If my experience with this other realm is something which we will eventually evolve to then there are some breathtaking leaps ahead in our development. I know because I've seen some of them.

Like many others exposed to the strangeness of the paranormal and unknown realities, I have sought ways to define what is going on. This is what anyone would do as a means to feel in control. The truth is I don't have any control and I am not sure anyone else in these circumstances really does. All I can possibly do in terms of empowerment is write about the things that have happened in the way I've interpreted them. That is what this book is about, my life's interaction with another side of reality. That doesn't specifically mean ghosts, UFO's or the legend of Atlantis and interaction doesn't necessarily mean being whisked away by aliens. It means something else on a deeply personal level that could be the common denominator to all these phenomena. Ideally it is about a personal interaction with something that I have come to call the "Otherness."

Writing about the presence of ghosts or extraterrestrials would be a lot easier but that would only add to the man-made definitions of the paranormal already there and not accurately tell my story. My encounters have been more of an alternative state of being than anything else, something which British paranormal researcher Jenny Randles has come to term the "Oz Factor." This is a silent dream-like state where birds, insects and everything around seem to be put on a still pause. It is where human consciousness will readily accept the bizarre just like dreaming Dorothy in the Wizard of Oz. Stage hypnotists love this state of being and can coax their subjects into doing almost anything as their conscious sense of critique is down and only sub-consciousness responds. It also explains how an advanced race of beings have managed to manipulate my mind into accepting the most outrageous scenarios without question, just like in a dream. I strongly suspect this is the method behind many of the reported UFO abductions.

So where exactly do we go when all this happens? The Otherness is all about that particular place, whether it be deep in the mind or on another plane of reality. I really don't have the answer to its location or its existence but I have been privileged to a fantastic insight of its mechanisms. It is a peculiar place, an understatement maybe.

This new state or place of being bears all the hallmarks of a dream, the inconsistency and the lucidity. The only difference being that something remarkably significant has actually taken place whereas a common dream would appear gobbledygook. The sleeping state appears to be remarkably significant and it seems to be the time when a subliminal or spiritual species prefer to interact. During the night I often slipped into an ancient realm which leaves me wondering why others already haven't. I am finally convinced of another zone that abductees and "out of body experiencers" are transported to in their hazy nocturnal hours. I've been to this place and it is fascinating.

In this book I will try to delve deeper into the stranger aspects of this zone and why the presence of its inhabitants appear so bizarre. I will explore why the agenda of visitors coming to this side of reality seem so cryptic and sometimes absurd. Above all I will demonstrate why the Otherness is about a secret life that I have unwittingly lived as well as being another side of the physical world that we think we know.

I have to begin by saying that my paranormal experiences have been quite different from most. I must reiterate that I cannot compartmentalise what has happened to me as a typical ghost case or UFO experience as my experiences seem to cover so many areas. What started with a strange memory followed by a UFO type encounter has triggered a shower of peculiarities ranging from déjà vu to some kind of parallel reality. Not even the Oz Factor can explain all.

This Oz Factor has proved to be far more than just a state of mind. For me it has become a gateway to an intangible and esoteric world which folklore calls "fairyland." Intangible in that I can never reach out and define it as an essential source of evidence. This of course leaves me without so much as a grain of proof and not a leg to stand on.

Even as I write, I feel myself wince at the absurdity of what I have to say. "These things just don't happen. How can I ever expect anyone to believe this?" And very little of it has actually taken place in the reality we're used to. Somewhere remote, it is all very real and has a solid significance. The significance is the mystery I call interaction, and again that is what this book is about. The "how" and the "why" behind it all is not really for me to say but I can at least try to translate the magic behind the Otherness and what you will see on these pages are my best interpretations.

Sometimes I feel like the Amazonian who has been given a fantastic glimpse of civilisation and actually approached it. My task now is to go back to the tribe and try to relay the strange tales of the new world. I am not an explorer of that world, rather I have been drawn or plunged into it and for some reason been granted the special privilege of memory. The inhabitants of that civilisation have allowed me to remember.

My memory is not the only rarity here. I can honestly say that none of my experiences have been unpleasant. Never have I encountered any threat or presence of evil on the other side. I have also never needed the valuable service of hypnotic regression, which is strange because I suspect my memory has often been tampered with. Because this has been such a deeply personal interaction and so cleverly disguised leaving no trauma whatsoever, there has been very little call for any investigation. There are very few people that I have actually approached and this I believe is rare.

I cannot approach people with these tales as it invariably leads to ridicule and denial. Denial probably being slightly sinister because it suggests that I have stumbled across something perennially dangerous that shouldn't be touched. I sometimes wonder if the same people who baulk are the ones who secretly fear or know there is more to life than we actually come across.

The esoteric beings that pull the strings to my life and many others want to leave as little trace or suspicion as possible. This allows a huge agenda free to carry on uninterrupted and there are many books on the paranormal that also suggest this. What concerns me is that it doesn't just limit itself to the stories of alien abductions. A secret agenda seems to apply also to haunting and outer body experiences just as if they are a part of the same tapestry.

In the past few years I have been reading up on religious histories as well as paranormal phenomena to try to shed some light on this strange and hidden study. It makes me wonder how much information we actually have about this institution and how much our ancestors really knew about it. Why have these things established themselves so well within our folklore? We just seem to live on with this accepted knowledge of our culture yet alarm bells only ring when we're confronted with something. Angels and aliens instantly strike me as something already known about from bygone days.

In my moments of strange interaction, I have met people who demonstrate things to me. Communication is always through the silent oddity that we call telepathy and gestures are made about things that certainly confuse. However, I am convinced that what was shown to me has a tremendous significance. So much of it is firmly anchored in our culture and smacks of familiar rituals that humans have carried out in our past. For instance, there is something about the ritual behind freemasonry and stage magic that has this uncanny resemblance to the bizarre ceremony I have witnessed. It seems that the powerful use of gesture goes hand in hand with these beings' telepathy and at times I have seen things which resemble magic wands, pointed hats, mysterious boxes and cloaked dwarfs. Despite the "Alice in Wonderland" type scenario, my experiences also have an ultra hi-tech theme that is straight out of tomorrow. I have seen the mythical world of wizardry used amongst technology to which our imaginations haven't yet stretched.

I am not from a cultural background that would favour any of these scenarios. Instead, I just take what I saw and relay it the best I possibly can. In fact, I believe there is a common bond that links everything paranormal. But does anybody really know why we use magic wands in conjuring and what the significance of the magician's box is? I suspect there are those that do.

I have often thought of this knowledge as institutional like a secret torch handed down from the keepers of ancient legend. It would explain our legacy of Masonic secrecy.

If this is a part of a hidden institution secretly passed down to "me" then the question is surely why? Where exactly do I fit in? I am not a part of any cult and possess nothing unusual in mind or body so the question screams, "why me?"

David Ike, the much-ridiculed sports commentator turned prophet and author of many spiritual- themed books was once posed exactly the same question on a television interview. Why had this mediocre sports presenter with little influence on the spiritual been chosen as a type of messianic prophet only to be the subject of endless jibes? His answer was a simple question. "Why was Jesus, a humble, unknown carpenter from Nazareth turned out to be mankind's saviour and the founder of the Christian religion?" In other words, why do bizarre and groundbreaking phenomena take place with the most unassuming people?

I am not claiming to be a messiah of any kind, but I will not be the first unknown to have had something strange happen to them. If there really were such privileges, then why not grant them to the Pope?

I don't think it works that way. I believe that a higher civilisation or race of beings have some kind of selection criteria but it isn't based on intelligence or spiritual development as some will have you believe. I do not want to mislead anyone into the condescension of New Age belief where only the highly developed achieve enlightenment. I for one have never meditated and probably have more materialist beliefs than most but what happened during my secret life is another matter.

It isn't that I have met with interplanetary beings or can prove there is an afterlife but my experiences have provided me with a strong suspicion that religion, New Age and science are not necessarily set in opposing quarters. Somewhere along the line they link hands quite naturally but the authority of each quarter will never let us see where. The beauty of not being from any of these backgrounds helps me see the whole phenomenon without bias. I can see why we thought of otherworldly beings as demons or angels hundreds of years ago and I can also see why we think of them coming from other planets today.

For me, I find science the best tool for interpreting the paranormal. It enables me to accept the phenomena at a grass roots level and seems to help explain the mechanisms behind religion without necessarily disputing it. I would love to be the first able to prove that the concept of an ethereal world is not as far away as people would believe and that you need not be a yogi to finally discover everything.

I am not an atheist but believe that maybe one day, God can be put under the microscope and that a high-tech medium will eventually propel us through the gates of Heaven. It is, after all, a growing awareness that helps us cross that line of taboo and allow the unknown to become known.

Like many others exposed to the paranormal, I have a strong feeling that those who monitor us, the angels, alien overlords, whatever are guiding us towards transformational changes like parents holding the baby as it learns to walk. This might mean that we are about to become "them", taking our place alongside the makers.

Something somewhere is preparing us gradually without our conscious minds being aware… but that is changing.

For the first time in evolution the cattle are becoming curious. They are venturing way outside of their field and what they are finding keeps them coming back for more until their knowledge becomes altered forever. The livestock are about to finally take their place amongst the farmers and this bizarre and ongoing harvest will no longer be a mystery.

1

The Secret Mould

I was always being prepared for something. Looking back, there was always this reserved suspicion that my history of interaction was actually a programme of some kind. This isn't something I can elaborate on; it's more a case of "knowing'.

Secret knowledge appears to be the bottom line for my experiences and has proved to be the cast that formed my interests. Reservoirs of untaught information are a common theme with alien interaction and in my case, it has been more of a way of life.

We accept the most bizarre things when growing up and only in our sober hindsight of adulthood do these things appear strange. I realise how the mind changes over the years along with our sense of reality but it doesn't explain why we sometimes instinctively have a fixed view towards something without even questioning it. If there's never been a known source for your influences, you can't help wondering where they came from.

I now know that the human mind can be programmed. I'm not talking about verbal influence or hypnosis but something far cleverer and more effective that causes you to hit a kind of boundary when you try to access it. Somebody has been programming my mind this way where I would simply go through my days believing that nothing is out of the ordinary and everything is the norm. I am going to refer back to this altered state called the Oz Factor because that I believe is where the "programmers" themselves operate.

An abductee can be halted at any time during the Oz Factor and sent into an altered state where everything happens in slow motion. It won't be until a much later stage that they realise something strange has happened along with missing time.

I believe that my programming has been even more advanced than this as I have grown up without suspicion. In fact, I haven't even been allowed the faculty of wondering because my firm belief always insists that the paranormal happens only to others. Again this was just an unquestioning mode of thought that didn't seem to come from anywhere. It wasn't until the programmers themselves decided one evening in early 1996 that I should finally remember. Prior to this, any level of strangeness belonged to the subconscious realm of dreams or the domain I called the Otherness.

Over the years I have learned a number of things about these programmers. As clever and advanced as they may be, their system is not without flaw. They obviously want a process as uninterrupted and free from suspicion as possible, but that isn't always the way it works. Look how many people who suspect missing time finally turn to hypnosis and reveal a huge chunk of the alien agenda. Look how many photographs and widespread stories of the paranormal have broken onto the news and onto bookshelves everywhere. Perhaps these people are only a handful of the experiencers existing. Thousands of others like myself may have participated in this way without being aware and will remain unaware indefinitely. I also suspect that the terrible leakage in the system coming from the outrageous minority making these claims have probably made their perpetrators tighten their belts. It would explain why my experience with these visitors have been even more stealthy and less like an alien involvement. Their ingenious method of inducing amnesia hasn't made me care to try hypnosis and not once have I ever (knowingly) been exposed to the archetype alien entity known as the "grey".

Pictures of these creatures don't strike a chord with me. That isn't to say that my version of events are correct and everyone else's are false, it just suggests that perhaps I am one of the first to witness a new or changing face of the paranormal. The fact that my experiences have never been unpleasant also suggests something very new indeed.

Maybe this is just a subjective thing. I often wonder if the inhabitants of the paranormal somehow prescribe different programmes for different subjects. What would appear as a malevolent grey brutalising some poor subject onto a higher fear threshold would deliberately appear quite differently to someone else. The more I read about other cases makes me appreciate just how different this interaction can be and just how fortunate I am. To be honest I am not as strong or brave a person as I would like and perhaps my threshold for stress is simply too low for that treatment. Perhaps the entities themselves are aware of this and have somehow offered a more sophisticated course of action where I would be totally oblivious to what is happening.

Even this extensive level of stealth offered to me has proved to have its leakages. There are hints of strangeness that have manifested themselves to me during childhood although not necessarily in an alien or paranormal way. It was more in the manifestation of my early ideas and interests that suggested something strange was going on. As a child I seemed to have interests and impressions that were never fed from anywhere.

Where did I acquire this early fascination for conjuring and magic when I had hardly seen it practiced anywhere? Why was I preoccupied with the notion of robed beings like monks who I believed carried out this magic? Why was a late developer like myself questioning the basic laws of physics at such an early age where I would spend hours with an electric torch wondering why I couldn't manipulate its light? Almost as if I'd seen it done somewhere. The night time occurrences were the strangest. I would often drift off to sleep with a series of numbers and advanced equations whizzing through my mind followed by the most vivid dreams of flying. Not the usual flying dreams that we all have but ones of being in complex machines.

Before I go into any depth about these, I need to reiterate the point I made earlier about the notion of being "selected." This isn't a privilege and I am not a celebrity or author who aims to take you on any New Age journey of enlightenment. This is the first book I have written and my convenient knack of explaining the unusual only comes from experience.

The truth is I am nobody. If the criteria for selection was based on sophistication, then I probably wouldn't have touched first base. In fact the life I thought I had led (the one I consciously remembered) was no more than a mundane legacy of under-achievement. I cannot remember any promising potential shining through as a child which would suggest I was destined for anything great. This book is largely about those two lives, the conscious one and the shrouded one revealed. I have found the contrast between the two to be quite breathtaking.

As the book continues, you will begin to see the reason for selection and what that criteria may be. I can assure you that it isn't something you have to slave at through personal development. Like most experiencers of the unusual will tell you, "it just happens."

The interactive experiences I have had were delivered to a lifestyle that was not particularly unique. I was born in the late sixties into a working class family living just outside of London. My father was a taxidermist and my mother a florist and although they were never poor, I remained an only child, possibly because it was manageable and partly for financial reasons. I think the social or financial category would have been upper working class, for me, however, I can only describe it as comfortable. I never went hungry or without anything and cannot claim the nobility of being poor.

Being an only child did contribute toward me developing into a loner, which is a trait I have to this day. From an early age I seemed to build up a resistance against loneliness or boredom by acquiring this strange world of my own. Like most children, I had imaginary playmates but these would occupy an unhealthy amount of my time. Today I am not so sure they were imaginary at all and I doubt children's creative abilities stretch that far.

Nevertheless, the activity kept me occupied and as always the interaction was pleasant enough to keep me coming back for more. Whatever it was I interacted with knew exactly what it was doing and had a lifelong agenda planned for me.

This hidden activity would prove to cause problems for me later on, particularly when I began school. Years later, a teacher described me as having too much activity going around in my head. I would often get into trouble for being miles away and "tuning out" at the most inconvenient moments. Being in a world of my own meant I would regularly get reprimanded by the teachers who at one point thought I was hard of hearing. I remember when I was about 7 years of age, a specialist was called into the school to test my hearing abilities. After a tedious test of repeating words spoken to me both clear and muffled without saying "pardon" once, it became obvious that there was nothing wrong. This led to the obvious pondering and humming adults do when pretending to understand. They could only diagnose me as being persistently "miles away" which was something that would follow me through my schooling and adult life.

Having a label of being a daydreamer would have been acceptable had there been some evidence of academic success to compensate for it. The trouble is, there wasn't, and within the black and white reasoning of children (and sometimes teachers) this meant quite plainly that you were thick. This stigma was worse as it led to a kind of despondency where I would opt out of studying and go further into my world of magic. My whole attitude to study eventually became one of "why bother," particularly when there was this head full of strange activity that made the absorption of new knowledge a huge task. I can remember times where I would find it agonising just to try to digest so much as a paragraph of a textbook when it didn't appeal to me. I could describe it as a bulimic mind: it simply wouldn't accept information, especially if that information didn't match what was within. If this was some fault of the aforementioned programming rather than just a lazy or feeble mind, then someone somewhere possesses some frightening uses of mind control.

Could I have had a separate education coming from elsewhere?

Having said all of this, there were times where my awkwardness would triumph and signs of this hidden world would prove to be an asset creatively. Whenever there was the opportunity to express my mind rather than develop it, people seemed to take notice. Writing stories from my own initial ideas was always a success at school and many times I would be asked to read my stories to the class. Looking back there were some funny ideas that I would incorporate into my writing which would baffle teachers and often myself. I seemed to have these preconceived ideas about how things were rather than the way they were factually. So many times I would be challenged on facts:

"But there aren't any monks who practice magic"

"Steel isn't organic like wood and cannot be grown, it has to be welded."

"How can you fly over the Earth without the use of a spacecraft?"

I would grow up dismissing these strange ideas as a part of my undisciplined imagination or as something odd from my dreams. What I wasn't aware of was that these ideas were developing more into fixations. Like most things, I kept them to myself and had learned the art of what not to say, particularly if it would alarm or embarrass.

Quite often they would manifest in my schoolwork and I found that teachers would either keep very quite about my odd theories or assume that I picked them up somewhere. This would happen when I was old enough to do science at school and had to write why you thought things were as they are. This first happened early in my secondary school during a particular exercise in the science lesson where we would be asked to write about a certain question, the answer to which remains unknown to this day. Something about why a multitude of different colours would always appear beige when spun around at a certain speed. I didn't really know the answer but I wrote something to the effect of "the light reaching you from the spinning object only allows you to see a vague combination of the primary colours while the others absorb into the speed of the wheel." This may have seemed a plausible, albeit advanced explanation for an 11 year old, but take into account I didn't really understand what I was saying.

The teacher didn't pursue this written theory although she casually remarked, "Who's your older brother doing physics in the fifth year?"

This alternative set of rules embedded in my mind appeared to have a particular theme to them that did not come from my culture. My fascination with stage magic and conjuring had come from my parent's practical trades, I assumed. From an early age I had wanted to be a stage magician and would often practice and play out the scenes in my bedroom. Again I would have preconceived ideas about how it should be done and what to expect. During these fantasy scenes I would be accompanied by a team of magical dwarfs who acted as my helpers and I would possess a metallic box that lead to a secret dimension. This was where all the conjuring would take place, the gateway to the ethereal world of spirits and goblins.

The vagueness I had about what to expect during my sessions of magic would often lead to frustration. Why didn't that just vanish and appear elsewhere? I'm sure I've seen it done somewhere. When I tried to process where it was that I'd seen it, my head would burn as if I approached a forbidden boundary. I knew that somewhere these tricks were performed using tools far more sophisticated than the plastic toys I had. Somewhere existed a world so strange that a mental taboo would crop up just by wondering about it.

Looking back, the fixations of my young mind appeared to have a pattern that was etched partly in what we know as folklore. There were cloaked beings that possessed the power of magic. This would explain my early fascination with the mystique of monks because that is what they dressed like. These beings carried out ceremonies that appeared slightly like the woodland solaces of Wicca people and not unlike the Masonic rituals of today. These "monks" would be accompanied by Troll-like people who were dressed the same only they were like assistants. What these ceremonies were for was something I could never fathom.

All of this remained as information etched in my mind about things that I believed existed, not necessarily something that actually involved me. Or at least I didn't think it did. For me it was just knowledge without a source and questioning its source would cause it to evaporate just like a fading déjà vu, the intricate work of "programmers."

They say that a little information is dangerous, which is why I learned to keep quiet about these beliefs early on. If you cannot explain how you know something then you really haven't a leg to stand on. Evidence is the factor that is seriously lacking in these occurrences.

In the event where my mind was allowed the capacity to question the scenarios, I would always come to the conclusion of dreams. That was it, vague memories of weird dreams, what else could they be?

Most of the time I am sure that dreams are only the resting mind's leisure time where it juggles information around with the dreamer's fears and imagination. There are the rare occasions however where something else happens between the sleep and waking state, where there is just too much lucidity and consistency for it to be a dream. The Oz Factor plays its part here and I believe it to be the habitat of peculiar entities.

These dreams were nothing of the kind. Just like the normal ones, they were easily forgotten and only recalled in vague patches later. This of course reinforced their invalidity. It makes me realise now how these shady entities have fooled so many over the years by manipulating the dream environment. I now understand the entities patterns and manoeuvres enough to be able to differentiate between the real and the non during the night encounters.

The "dream people" of my childhood were different. The ones that came at night were different from the "monk magicians" and seemed to display ultra technology rather than magic. I always knew when I was about to have one of the "night people" dreams because the environment around me changed. I didn't necessarily need to be asleep either. A kind of oppressive atmosphere would fill the room just before a visit and the sounds around me such as the downstairs television or the toilet flushing became distant as if underwater. The interaction always followed on after a mental cascade of numbers which meant nothing to me.

Once this had happened I was in the night people's realm, the ethereal and immaterial existence I call the Otherness. Changes would also take place in me as I was physically different. Once in this state I could do the things they did such as float or converse telepathically without questioning the phenomena. I would often be taken from my bed and led on some abstract journey. Ludicrous and incredible.

My young mind often assumed these beings were children because of their size, but when I think back to their actual appearance I realise of course that they weren't. They had all the filled out characteristics of an adult although they couldn't have been much more than 4 feet high. Their appearance was humanlike although not exactly. In fact they resembled dolls with their perfectly proportioned features and smooth skin, so much so that they couldn't have been human. Another ironic feature they had was "painted on hair" just like some of the action dolls I played with at the time. They had to have been dolls; their mouths were in a fixed position when they spoke to me without sound.

Each of them wore a jumpsuit, sometimes in an orangey brown colour and other times a dull grey but what each of them had always was uniformity, all in brown or all in grey. I found that they usually arrived in fours, sometimes more depending on the operation at hand.

The interesting thing was that I never recalled how they would enter my bedroom. They would somehow manifest. I would just wake up to find a suffocating presence in the room together with a dim light that seemed to come from nowhere with the beings themselves gently coaxing me out of bed for a task for which I was always strangely prepared. Very little communication took place but when it did, it was never demanding. Non-verbal words of reassurance were occasionally spoken in ways which adults reassure children.

I would then simply float with them as each held me the way a lifeguard might when teaching someone to swim. Sometimes the atmosphere in the room felt so thick it was almost like being in water and although my physical form was still humanoid, its properties were different. I suspect that we have an "in-between state" somewhere amidst the physical and astral that is definitely astral in form but borrows all the human anatomy. I will go into this "halfway state" in more detail at a later chapter.

The form that I adopted with the night people allowed me to pass through solid objects much like a radio wave. I can remember always passing through a hole in the ceiling (which was never there in the morning) and actually feeling the texture of the ceiling around me. Wherever we went or whatever we passed through, the same dim bluish light would follow like an encompassing halo. When we reached the outside, things were not quite as expected. In theory we should have been above the rooftop of my house overlooking the trees and facing the nearby motorway. Instead we were inside a cave of some kind illuminated only by the dim halo that followed us. There were steps that led down to a parked vehicle positioned on a kind of rail track as if it were a funfair ride ready to board. I could never remember getting inside that car but once inside, it didn't feel as though it actually moved. Instead, the scenery would change around us as images would fade and emerge until the backdrop suddenly became consistent. It would always be a struggle to remember what happened at this stage but I seem to recall being shown things around me.

The vehicle itself I am almost embarrassed to explain, because immediately it reminded me of something. I remember it being a flat silvery car without any edges and no roof above it. Its seating area only came up to the level of our chests (remember, I only had the height of a 7 year old) and I don't remember feeling any wind pass us as we flew, assuming that's what we did. The car travelled without sound and was so similar to the comic book flying vehicle known as the "Fantasi-car" from the superhero strip the "Fantastic Four." As reluctant as I am to divulge it this way, it is how I clearly remembered it and conveying it any different would be fabrication.

I think some things are so absurd in the abduction scenario that people often do modify their stories in order to sound sane!

The absurdity was the main factor that made me doubt all of these events as dreams over the years. Why would these beings need a vehicle to fly anyway when they could fly themselves? I have often heard stories of how victims of alien abduction sometimes suspect that the beings themselves are using illusions or play scenes in order to mask the reality of the abduction. I couldn't grasp what was so secretive about this flight scene that would make my visitors want to mask it as a scene from an American comic book! Despite the absurdity, I'm pretty sure I am remembering it the way it was. Perhaps the Fantasi-car is just another illusive vehicle alongside the flying saucer, I really couldn't say.

That would be the extent of my memory with the night people and their excursions. It didn't necessarily bring me any closer to them or their world. Questions remained unanswered— weren't even asked. The programmers had kept me safe in a non-curious state of mind. By morning, the strange events with the night people were no more than patches of a shady but familiar dream. There were peculiar occasions however where I would awake with physical evidence of the dream. For instance, I would find blades of grass in my bed the morning after dreaming of being in a field with the night people. Although I could never understand this, it didn't make me any more suspicious. I would go about my business in the normal way still believing that my life was as mundane as any schoolboy's.

Every day I would travel to school on that well-worn bus dreaming about the far reaches of space and time, thinking how insignificant my life was compared with this subject of interest. Connecting these interests with my own life and its strange moments had never really occurred.

That did not mean that my mind would ever cease its strange fixations. In fact they cropped up fast and furious. My written stories at school would continue to have the most baffling themes and theories, which the teachers were now starting to expect. They had soon put it down to too much television and at the time I suspected they might have been right. But I couldn't relate my ideas to anything that I had seen on TV or anywhere for that matter. It all seemed to point to a "secret education" coming from somewhere that a boy of my age could never normally access. It would explain much of the bizarre activity going on in my head around that time that was causing me to flunk most subjects. The activity generated within didn't seem to allow for much relevant information to be fed. It was causing notable failure.

At the back of my mind, there seemed to be an unexplainable consolation about my academic failure. It was like a distant a voice telling me not to worry, "You know what you're really here for." This went back to the almost arrogant notion of "being selected" and had I ever questioned this calling, I'm sure it would have responded to the effect of "some day it will all make sense." It was an inbred notion that all of this unpleasant underachievement was just the rocky road to something big.

The transition to secondary school and adolescence didn't bring me any closer to an answer. The bane of under-achievement followed me still and any possible building blocks for an academic career looked pretty unlikely. My unusual interests and pre-occupations were however growing into something.

I was becoming increasingly interested in the paranormal and often wondered why I hadn't come across anything unusual when I was convinced it existed. There was a magazine around at the time called the Unexplained which I read with fascination. Each month I waited in anticipation for the next issue to read up on strange accounts of ghostly experiences and extraterrestrials. Although I never knew where this intrigue came from, I seriously felt I could relate to the stories being told, particularly ones of meetings with strange beings. I tended to skip past the formalities of reports such as sightings and physical evidence and home in on the more intriguing aspects such as the personal experiences. These would entail stories of outer body journeys and actual alien abductions. The stories of personal interaction would never fail to keep me glued to the magazine, taking in every detail.

During that time there was the famous case in Yorkshire of a man found dead on top of a coal heap as if mysteriously placed there from above. He had been slain by some unknown burns as if from radiation and to corroborate this story, there was also the case of a local policeman claiming to have been abducted by a UFO around the same time. This account was a fascinating one brought into clarity through hypnosis where the man claimed to have been aboard an unknown craft lying on an operating table surrounded by small robot-like beings examining him.

At times like this I would seriously ponder over the meaning of it all and wonder if a mass landing was ever going to take place. I often wondered if we were ever getting nearer to a final revelation of the unknown, God, even? What would be the outcome of this and would it tell us what happens when we die? I always harboured this strong suspicion that these phenomena were all related.

My young mind could only guess what it might be about and my ideas were of course tainted with popular science fiction. Without the help of these "programming beings" of whom I wasn't aware at the time, this fancy proved to be a damaging tool to mask my experiences and keep them from my daily life. I would never equate my fascination with the unknown to personal experience as long as I thought of it in terms of robots and laser beams. Years would pass before I outgrew my insistence that the paranormal was all about Star Trek.

As a child, the nearest I would ever come to seeing an unknown object in the sky was something that we as a family all witnessed and still joke about today. It must have been about 1981. One winter's evening my parents and I were having dinner when we saw a green fireball whiz through the sky heading towards Heathrow. My father jokingly pointed up, saying, "Look, UFO!" knowing of course my fascination with the subject. We were so used to seeing fireworks around that time that we quickly dismissed the green flash as another sky-rocket; although, for a firework, it was unusual. The object made no sound and had a brilliant green consistency to it. Later that evening, a bulletin came over on the radio that dozens of reports had come in of a mysterious green fireball in the sky over London. I suspected it was a comet, but years later when I would read so much literature on UFOs, I read something about a government project known as Project Twinkle. This project was set up in the 1950s to study the mysterious green fireballs seen across America around that time. As intriguing as it all seemed, I have to conclude coincidence on that one. I strongly doubt that it had anything to do with my experiences. In hindsight I find it amusing how inappropriate this sighting must have been for those who I suspect were involved with me.

Intrigue would always remain together with the strange fixations. There was something about the image of Earth as seen from space that would always strike a note with me. Whenever I saw NASA's photographic images of our planet on television, I would immediately observe and feel a strange familiarity with something. Had I seen this once already other than TV?

This suspicion went back to an early age. My parents remember that when we would watch footage of the space explorations on TV how I, at age three or four, would point to the black and white images and say that I had seen that big globe before. Quite innocently, they would insist that it was our world seen from space and only astronauts see that. I would remark that I had seen it and it was bigger!

There is something about the striking image of Earth that moves me even today. I seemed to recall images of a huge section of a blue glassy marble-like structure beneath me. All around was dark but the fantastic surface that I looked upon was illuminated in the most majestic way. My programmers must have had a job erasing this scene from my mind because its brilliance grabbed me and always will. I was so in awe of this image that it could have been a living entity talking to me, like a collective message from its billions of inhabitants. Even though I never connected this scene with my interest in the paranormal, I don't think I ever dismissed it as a dream either. This had to have happened; it was so lucid and intricate.

Like most scenes, I can only remember snapshots and never the sequence of events that brought me there. My memories seemed to capture images and emotions and I feel that the gargantuan globe could have been an entity living and breathing with me. The scene was powerful and more than just a visual thing.

This snapshot recall of events has taught me a lot about the realm of existence I call the Otherness. It has been noted that those who experience the Oz Factor often come across a feeling of time slowing down or even put on a still pause on time itself. This slow motion or seizure of events can appear at anytime. Remember how it is when a sudden accident takes place like dropping a tray full of food in a busy canteen? You almost watch it happen in slow motion or even experience déjà vu as you helplessly see it happen. I suspect that the operating realm of the Programmers is a kind of timeless zone where the past, present and future are all an abstract scene of things happening at once. It is hard to imagine this timeless zone with our law of physics but it would account for the high (sometimes illogical) level of strangeness in which these visitors operate.

The still pause of life is another of the many ludicrous ideas I had from an early age that seemed to come from nowhere but within. As a child, I would ponder over the boundaries of the universe as many children do, wondering where it all could possibly end. Surely if there was a boundary, there must be something outside that boundary and if was limited, what was it that limited it? From a young age I concluded that the universe might be confined by a boundary in time where time as we experience it simply stops ticking. A place where there cannot be a before and after or a "here" or "there." When people talk of doing things in "no time", my theory of a simultaneous universe or timeless zone soon comes to mind.

This could just have been the way my young mind rationalised the common and frustrating puzzle of space and time. As I mentioned earlier, perhaps our minds were not designed to solve these problems. It was a theory that really meant something to me, a subject I could have talked about for hours. I remember comedy sketches from television shows such as Benny Hill where he would use a video's remote control to still pause time and events around him. I often mused at how effective this would be in travelling trillions of miles in "no time'. Going through a zone devoid of time or distance. This all sounds similar to the idea that modern scientists have of "tachyons" and "bending space/time." It also smacks of the Oz Factor and would allow a perfect environment for the aliens themselves to operate without so much as a hint of disturbance. It also reminds me of my absolute confusion about missing time and its sequence of events.

God only knows how many of these bizarre events have taken place in my life during this altered state where I explore the Otherness. I had the most profound snippets of memory that conveyed nothing to me but confusion. All I really knew deep down was the notion of "being prepared." Sometimes I felt like the wholesome calf being nurtured as a delicacy for the future or whatever the harvest was. The truth was deliberately spared from me, and in hindsight, the Programmers must have shown an element of kindness in doing that. Even if the grand master plan was benevolent, I'm not sure how my young and obsessive mind would have coped with the information. Perhaps I would have been a nervous wreck today.

Being prepared meant a meticulous process and unfortunately this did very little for my material needs and future. Sometimes when I look back, I must have drifted through those years as a zombie because I cannot seem to account for the way time flew. The process didn't leave room for any other essential developments and this left me quite maladjusted.

The important years of preparation for a decent future were being neglected and for some reason I didn't seem to care. Some other project was subconsciously taking place all the time and my studies were just a type of supplement to top up this secret project. I realised that a crucial time was looming with final exams on the horizon and necessary qualifications for the future but even acknowledging this importance didn't alter things. I felt indifferent to it all. My secret activity of hooded monks and night people with their ceremonies of magic and bizarre science seemed to take precedence of everything. In fact it was the real world that seemed the odd one.

I didn't think it necessary to apply for my final examinations because sitting them would have been futile. Apart from the core subjects, the rest of the exams were optional and required payment. I declined them all because I was nowhere near prepared. This ill preparation had followed me right into the outside world and shaped me as the proverbial square peg in an unsympathetic system of round holes.

My early ambitions of going into performing and becoming a stage magician had seemed to have dried up. The intrigue of conjuring had never really faded. I had become disillusioned with the conventional ways of going about it. It wasn't so much the trickery behind magic that appealed to me, it was the magic itself. When I was old and wise enough to know that the appearance of magic was just trickery, something inside me just didn't seem to buy it. Instead of conventional stage magic, my attention shifted towards the performed feats that couldn't be explained such as telepathy and spoon bending.

I hadn't abandoned my interest in performing altogether as I had continued with drama at school which I seemed to have a knack for. With drama there were no hard and fast rules about how it should be done and I seemed to shine in the art of portraying other people. I wondered sometimes if this was due to my lacking personality or the belief that the lives of others were far more exciting. It did feel like a refreshing escape at the time and above all, it was fun.

When it was finally time to depart those school gates, I realised I wasn't going straight into the theatre. However, I enjoyed being in that make believe environment so much that I had to seek some kind of role there even if it was stagehand. I collected the occasional stage magazines and looked for opportunities at any level. I did eventually arrive in the theatrical world albeit at the very menial levels. This at least provided me with a platform in which to drift from position to position without ever really going anywhere. I shifted scenes, I helped out with basic maintenance of the stage but as far as the make believe world was concerned, I was an onlooker.

At the end of the day, the secret obsessions had dictated the kind of maladjusted life that I had secretly feared. School may have been behind me forever, but that unforgettable label of "hopeless dreamer" from my school reports had prevailed.

I would remain for a very long time without a direction. Halfway through my twenties I remained without a clue of who I really was or what I was cut out for. The crazy mind full of bizarre activity had never truly been addressed as I had only accepted the flippant diagnosis others had given me.

The only reassurance I harboured was the deep suspicion of being selected, being prepared for some great task. No logic I had could explain it. There was nothing to support the belief. My future seemed vacant and my purpose was like putty in the hands of others who were quite out of reach for human evidence. There were those who truly had me where they wanted me and it wouldn't be until a later stage, after a series of bizarre interactive experiences, that an explanation would finally loom.

2

A Leak in Pandora's Box

If there was one thing that astounded me about the Programmers, it was their ability to induce amnesia. I would never have believed how a sensitive and conscious person like myself with a marked interest in the occult could have been shrouded all these years without so much as an inkling.

There were still fragments of memory which didn't seem to fit my life in any way at all. Much of them were of technology, others of magic and nearly all of them were of the familiar "magic monks" of my childhood.

Had there ever been a master plan right from the beginning, I suspect a destined breakthrough would at least be in the cards some time in the future. Then there would be answers. It was now 1994 and the lifelong yarn of hazy memories and bizarre dreams had suddenly started to take shape, albeit prematurely.

For some reason, memories of seemingly uninteresting events from my past were striking back at me with a new clarity, revealing far more than I would have ever recalled. There was a particular time I remember at the age of about twelve or thirteen when I was taken ill once during school. I briefly remember being ushered into the medical room and left there to recover.

Something about the event was unusual because at the time I seriously believed my illness was far worse than the staff at school had recognised. I vaguely remember laying there wondering why on earth they had left me. That was it as far as my conscious memories were concerned. I don't even recall going back to normal lessons that afternoon but obviously I did.

Years had passed and that dull incident hadn't even crossed my mind any more. It wasn't until thirteen years later, one evening in bed when drifting off to sleep (a common time for flashback memories) when something struck me about the event that I hadn't thought of in years. The robed beings and everything, how did I ever manage to forget that. I sat up in bed with a jolt, recalling the true version of the incident and feeling gobsmacked as to why it had never occurred this way before.

From what I remembered, it was one of those "free for all" lessons where pupils leisurely caught up with their homework, etc., and I recalled feeling quite peculiar for most of that morning. The pinnacle of that strange feeling arrived during this lesson and I remember reporting it to the supervising teacher before nearly passing out. I cannot recall being taken down to the school medical room but I do remember being there with a number of teachers and the school nurse around me. As I lay there I remember hearing the occasional comment like "he has a temperature" and "it's the first time this one's been taken sick" and feeling relieved that they recognised it. A strange thing followed after I heard them say that I should "just get some rest" and decided to leave me to recover. I was simply too weak to protest and just lay there hearing the door close behind them. The deep sleep I plunged into was second to none but when I came round, things were not as I had expected.

My first thoughts were "why have they moved me? This wasn't the room I was taken to, if fact I wasn't even sure this was the school. Had I been taken to hospital?

The room didn't strike me as medical. It was more like a cave of some kind composed out of wax with a familiar light that came from nowhere. Even the bed that I laid on was different, like it was filled with gel that seemed to mould to my very shape. I had never felt so comfortable. It seemed I wasn't alone, either. Someone was behind me doing something to my head.

"How come we changed rooms?" I remember asking.

There was no reply. I noticed that the figure behind me was wearing a hood which I thought was strange. My instant reaction was that it was a doctor wearing a type of germ protection, something like a surgeon's mask. Had my condition become so serious that I was having an operation? I noticed that the figure also had company that seemed to stand there and observe his movements like trainee doctors. I had the impression that these beings, however many there were, were evasive of being looked at. I asked another question. "Am I allowed to look at you?"

There was a pause but this time the "doctor" of the group responded. "You're allowed to, but you mustn't get frightened any more."

His answer was surprising. I wasn't frightened, more quizzical than anything. My impression of being moved to a special ward seemed to have made a lot of sense but I still couldn't understand where those teachers went and who these people were if not teachers or doctors.

"You knew how ill I was, why did you all leave me like that?" As soon as I said this I knew I was addressing the wrong people. The reply, however, was fascinating because it now makes me realise that telepathy must have been used. They simply knew what I was referring to.

"You can always trust them to do that can't you?"

I'm not sure if that was the exact reply but it was something to that effect. His answer had shown a bit of levity which I homed in on. I later learned how effective this form of communication can be as there can never be any misunderstandings. I suspect emotions are conveyed with their language and every message and gesture is properly received without saying "pardon".

Sometimes questions are answered before they even leave your mouth. For instance, while he was doing something to my head from behind, I still kept wondering where I actually was. I hadn't wondered for long because one of the being's small helpers walked round to me to demonstrate something. My first thought was that it was a fellow pupil dressed in a robe because of his size but my attention was immediately drawn to an object in his hand that he presented to me. I sat up and examined the object which appeared to be one of those bowl-like toys that children play with, the ones filled with clear liquid that display a scene when you shake them—a snow globe. This was very similar in size and shape and was also filled with clear liquid only there was no moveable scene inside. Things seemed to happen when I moved it.

The liquid inside was not as clear as I thought it might be, but a cascade of colours that were created just by slight movement. It wasn't long before pictures were forming. I couldn't believe that I was actually looking at a three-dimensional image of the cave type room we were in. As I viewed the crystal from above, I saw an aerial view of the room with an image of three brown robed beings examining a boy which I was fascinated to find was me. As I viewed the object from its side, I would see another angle and so on.

This was the most convincing hologram I had ever seen because even our own versions are normally on flat objects and never real enough not to be able to decipher. I mean I could have actually believed there were tiny beings in that crystal moving around. The choice of image also seemed to depend on movement and as I tilted it further, the scene would shift to another one in seconds. The liquid would blacken and then out of nowhere came a new scene. I remember seeing a number of different images in this crystal that I couldn't recognise, one of them being an image of outer space. I didn't know what any of this was supposed to mean to me but I surmise it might have been a way of demonstrating where I actually was. First the examining room and then goodness knows where.

The object was truly mesmerising. It could do things I had never seen. I remember turning it at all angles trying to get the picture of myself in the room, but it was unable to "tune in" to that again. It was all simply too much.

I remember the being taking back the object and saying (conveying) something to the affect of "does that answer your question?" Following this was the familiar confusion I have about "sequence of events". Everything happening afterwards seemed to take place in the jumbled "fast-forward" mode. I briefly remember something demonstrated to me, a magical feat of some kind using that familiar box. I never seem to remember what happens with this box and often wonder if it's some sort of amnesia device as it's always the last thing I see. It seemed to be a reminder that the session was about to come to an end. Just looking at it would bring about the familiar grogginess where everything became distant.

The whole memory of this strange event from years gone by faded as I sat there mesmerised in my bed.

I almost begged for the image not to fade on me that evening in 1994. There I was, sitting up in bed in utter disbelief at a dim memory that I had kick-started without warning. Only seconds ago I was drifting off into a peaceful sombre, the type I usually have to struggle to achieve. The serene images that usually accompany this state were taking shape and then, like a slap to the face with a cold and damp hand, the sudden memory of that seemingly irrelevant day in the school medical room appeared. It seemed like an unthinkable accident on the Programmers' part for allowing me to glimpse that forgotten occasion. As odd as it was, I wasn't going to let go.

I remember getting out of bed and immediately putting the light on. I had to walk around for a bit just to let my mind recollect the incident that I believed happened back in 1981, totally different to the way I remembered it.

I remembered feeling sick and dizzy that particular afternoon and had to be taken to the school medical room. Two teachers and a nurse briefly took my temperature and left me there to sleep it off. I remember sleeping without a trace and waking up later feeling better than ever! I returned to lessons that afternoon and thought no more about it.

However, I always remembered having conversations afterwards that didn't seem to fit. When asked, I remember telling classmates bizarre tale about the incident that I knew weren't true. Something about being cured by my secret comrades, the magic monks who visited me at school using a crystal ball. I normally wouldn't have said these things as it would have guaranteed ridicule or just be seen as flippancy. Although I do remember having some intrigue about that medical room afterwards and regularly sneaking in there during break time to investigate. I must have been desperately searching for that secret cave or whatever it was, the place with the soft and source-less light. Nothing at all, just the usual bland interior of the school medical room with its rubbery bed and light green curtains.

It wasn't the first time I had been disappointed by secret locations that proved not to hold any clues. It was similar to my belief about the magic hole in my bedroom ceiling that I regularly passed through with the night people. Nothing was ever there by morning. The strange hangar that housed the uncanny space vehicle of the night was never on the other side of the ceiling either, just the same old slate tiling of my rooftop. The magical cave of the school medical room was just another example. There seemed to be a consistent theme here about the subject of disassociation cropping up regularly in my incidents and a few other cases I've read about. Why is it that things are sometimes noticeably out of place, almost like there is another version of them similar to the physical but not exactly? I realise how this smacks of the dream scenario and reinforces the notion that perhaps they were all simply dreams but that's exactly the point of my suspicion - the "dream software" seems to be used for accessing this strange territory. These experiences are far too real to be dreams yet they aren't exactly like the physical either.

Getting back to sleep was going to be impossible that night. Too much had come flooding back and even then as I paced the room, I could feel something frantically trying to withdraw the memory. I struggled not to let it go, it was just like trying to recollect the familiar glimpses of fading déjà vu. Something somewhere was trying to restrain my emotions by pumping in denial before I had a chance to process the notion of a UFO type abduction. Yet that is what it seemed like, a medical examination at a young age by non-classified beings, the phenomena that I was convinced I had no part of. Whenever I tried to think of the incident this way, my head would start to burn, telling me I had crossed the forbidden boundary. I wasn't going to retreat this time because I was sure I had something. Somewhere in the past I had been subject to a paranormal presence and this taboo boundary had to be explored.

The sudden illness of that particular day and the presence of the brown robed beings were key features of something in my life that never added up. It certainly accounted for my life-long interest in magic and folklore especially with that viewing device. What else could that have been if it wasn't some kind of Gypsy crystal ball? It changed colour. I saw images inside and even remember glimpsing a picture of outer space. The monks themselves had shown me a box which could easily have passed as the legendary tinderbox used in magic to make things vanish. This event just screamed of everything I suspected about folklore and science and what I believed to be the foundation of my obsession.

This was a breakthrough. I couldn't contain myself. A voice in the distance bellowed at me, insisting that it was only a dream but the familiar denial wasn't washing. In fact I now recognised the denial as part of a phenomena that didn't necessarily come from me. All these years it had won over by masking any of the oddities with a type of programme. My own free will and critical sense now challenged that programme and it was making my head feel as though circuits were malfunctioning. Regardless of the slight burn and the confusion that accompanied it, I tried to focus on nothing but that incident at school. My single-minded thinking that night was finally helping me to make that breakthrough.

The following few days were equally peculiar. Life would never be the same. As suspected, I didn't sleep that particular night but instead slept for most of the following morning. My pattern and lifestyle were changing and that day, my dreams took on an unusual and bizarre form. I remember reading many cases from UFOlogy where abductees were warned through dreams to forget incidents. Alien entities have been known to penetrate dreams. This is a phenomenon that dates back even further than our folklore. Wasn't there an event featured in the Bible during the period of Christ's birth where a warning was delivered in the form of a dream? The dream environment seemed to have been "their" territory where interaction could comfortably be carried out without interruption.

Now that my visitor's programme had accidentally malfunctioned one particular night, I had at last been spared an insight into their strange manoeuvres. I had obviously seen too much. Rather than Pandora's Box being opened and being saturated with its wealth of information, I had instead been exposed to just a glimpse when the lid briefly lifted. The Greek legend has it that this box was filled with hope and I would no doubt become hungry for more of that hope and it would be much harder to return to the blissful ignorance I once enjoyed.

A series of incidents occurred in which I would keep waking and drifting off again only to plunge into the most cryptic dreams. It felt as though I kept being summoned to their realm and its strange system of illusions and play scenes. In the dreams, the "warners" would sometimes take the form of familiar people and then of something more bizarre. I dreamed of a type of committee of non-human beings addressing me with messages I could never remember. These beings were like magicians possessing the ability to masquerade as anyone that my mind conceived. Yet even in the dreams, I possessed enough free will to resist their demands. From what I remember, the committee were urging, pleading with me to discard my new memories because I "just wasn't ready for the information behind them." I on the other hand fought to seize the knowledge I had of that episode because I knew there was untold information like that ready to be hatched from other events of my life. I knew that something had been responsible for all of my peculiarities and that these beings and their hidden episodes like the medical room were a vital key. Their failed attempts of dissuasion kept luring me back for more.

I had discovered what it means to have recurring and continuing dreams. For the next few nights, the secret ethereal committee would continue to plague me but it seemed that a certain subconscious defiance would have none of it. I was burning for more information and felt on a high. There was always my natural fascination with the paranormal and now that I had a bee in my bonnet about actually being a part of it, nothing could really stop me. I suspect the Programmers knew this and realised what a problem they had on their hands altering this programme. In the dreams, the warnings would border on threats and often accompany strange visual displays which demonstrated how "un-ready" I was. I would be shown scenes of myself cracking up under the new information exposed. Accompanying the scenes were narrations of how I should pursue different interests in life and steer clear of anything strange. It was all extremely vivid but I suspect, for the first time, the Programmers were unable to exert total control.

Aside from the dreams, there were many daytime oddities taking place. In fact there were irregularities in my whole being that pointed to something strange going on. My mind seemed to have become an activity zone for déjà vu and these sensations were coming fast and furious. I would never quite remember the actual nature of these déjà vu experiences as they always deteriorate quickly but I later decided to take note. I had developed a bizarre list that seemed to point to all kinds of things ranging from non-classified humans and animals to events.

There were also hints of psychic energies developing that would manifest uncontrollably. At work there were times when I would walk passed desks and paper documents would fly off and follow me, sticking to my back as though I carried a static. This would have seemed plausible had it happened only once or twice particularly as people are known to pick up static occasionally but this was different. The effects were quite dramatic, even poltergeist-like. Also it would only happen when I was unaware and if I tried to incite the effect deliberately, it never worked.

My interaction with people also took a strange turn as I had become extra intuitive of how they felt and what their thoughts might be. These effects seemed to cause my emotions to mimic theirs and it left me wondering why

I felt certain things without any reason. When they were down, I would feel that way also. It was as though their state of mind left an atmosphere in the room that I would unintentionally feed off of. I remember one particular work colleague during this time who had gone out of her way to avoid me ever since that phase had begun. She was a temp worker who like me was on contract at the theatrical management company where I worked. Long after I had left I learned that she was actually into psychic studies and possessed some sort "gift" from an early age. From another colleague I discovered that she had "sensed" something strange about me, ever since a particular given time which just happened to be the time of my new discovery. I was apparently giving her the creeps and she felt that I was looking right into her soul.

During this period I was living with my fiancé and so many times we would have what's known as mutual dreams. I would wake the following morning and recite the dreams I had which tallied 100% with hers. It was peculiar situations like these that took a toll on our relationship and even though I remained on this high, my old reserved self still kept the strange recent developments a secret. Like everyone else, she remained blissfully unaware.

My lifelong tendencies were difficult enough to live with aside from the possibility that I might be involved with something unknown. I no longer brought up the subject of mutual dreaming because it obviously offended her, understandably so. It was this strangeness and the tendencies of a double life that eventually caused this relationship to crumble and others that followed. My loner instincts were causing bad social habits and I was starting to refer to this Otherness not just as a term for another existence but for my life also. There were so many undercurrents going on that I was losing track of who I actually was. A hidden life was desperately trying to remain that way because of intangible forces at work.

It would have been fair to say that the dream scenario had infringed upon my waking hours and any confidence I had about reality was slowly withdrawing. I felt no fear, only frustration because I knew this was being done outside my control. There were times during this period that I would doubt or forget obvious things and be unable to decipher the real from the unreal, almost like Alzheimer's disease.

My belief system was being toyed with and at times it became very clear why. There were mornings where I would awake believing that this whole revelation was just a huge misunderstanding and I should just forget about it. I must admit, I felt a certain comfort in that belief, but knew deep down it wasn't mine. These conflicting feelings would cause me to swing to extreme opinions ranging from sceptic to believer. During the doubting moods I knew the Programmers were winning, yet there would always be that glimpse of truth in the background that insisted something was going on.

The conflict continued. There were times when the presences of others were more prominent—the moments between wake and sleep. On the rare occasion where I might drift off such as on train or car journeys, the dozing state would take off with a distant voice summoning me. It wasn't an unpleasant summoning, more like a parent trying to get the attention of a distracted child. Occasionally my mind would process a face to this voice and when I think of it, I could get a focused picture if I wanted to. I have never been hypnotised but the lucidity I experienced in this halfway state seemed to be the nearest I would come. In fact, the elaborate detail I picked up during my dozing moments was sharper than my conscious perceptions.

The face I saw when I chose to examine the voice's source was a familiar hooded being. It wore the brown monk's habit that made it resemble one of those robed dwarf creatures in the first Star Wars film. When I chose to home in on the face under the hood, I gained an intricate picture, of which I could have produced a useful portrait of had I been given a pencil. Although I never considered this being to be evil, the face that I glimpsed certainly wasn't pleasant. In fact it was so wrinkled and debauched that had I put an age to it I would have gone well beyond a human life expectancy. It was how I would imagine a corpse to have looked months after its decease and its off white colour certainly gave that impression. The wrinkles hardly allowed the eyes to be visible but what I saw were weathered slits that must have seen centuries go by. I often wonder if it was a living corpse in a shroud I was looking at. Had I have witnessed this person in any other state I would have been undoubtedly scared. The twilight consciousness is an effective, fascinating place to be in and I can see why the Programmers have hijacked it for their own use.

The being told me things I could never remember afterwards. There were unrecalled conversations between us where his voice was clear without lips moving and mine was also present without speech. Whatever was said, I think I protested. I remember trying to keep the dream consistent and see how far it would go without consciousness creeping in. Whenever the slightest fear or doubt came into the scene, my critical sense would rudely return awakening me with a jolt.

Memories washed away and I returned to my old self. I often suspected that a delicate communication link was broken when this happened as I always knew it was never just a dream.

I also suspect that the Programmers tried all sorts of desperate tricks to interact with me at all possible opportunities. The manifestations of these attempts seemed alien to me in all senses of the word. Nothing was ever direct and the scenarios were always abstract.

The dreams continued and appeared to be taking a different form. These unconscious liaisons with the "monks" were just as frequent although I was starting to pick up extra memories of the dream. The monks came in threes most times, the same particular three it seemed. This was a facet that I wasn't aware of before. Also when I tried to think of where all this took place, the dreamscape looked like a desert somewhere with a backdrop of sand dunes and a sunset. Three robed beings, one of which appeared to be the leader, set in a type of desert with conversational debates that I don't clearly remember. What did any of this tell me?

There were other vivid and striking dreams also that appeared more relevant than the others. These were dreams of a night sky occupied with the most breathtaking craft which could only have been recognised as UFO's. I would stand there absolutely spellbound looking up at a night sky filled with these strange craft with no knowledge of where I was or who piloted these objects. In the dream, these UFO's didn't appear to be the classical cigar-shaped objects or the newer triangular ones but a design more akin to something from centuries ago, gothic even. The craft appeared enormous, bigger than anything reported so far and had a design more like medieval castles than hi-tech ships. I remember the craft in all shapes and sizes but each of them were soundless with a ghostly blue white light and some were slightly transparent. I have no sequential memories of these dreams, just the awesome image of this fantastic gothic looking craft taking up the entire backdrop of sky.

Years later I would see similar photographs of these craft from a book about the famous Gulf Breeze sightings in Florida in the late eighties. The snapshots were quite fantastic and very similar to the craft I had actually dreamt about although not exactly. The mysterious blue glow was there together with the look that wasn't unlike something gothic and the similarity from my dreams did ring a bell. The dreams I had however displayed images so lucid and unique that I would have trouble comparing them with anything I had seen. I recalled these craft having old-fashioned cogs or wheels that appeared to rotate the ship's exterior slowly as it moved through the sky. There was a type of inconsistency where the texture of the ship's surface would move, stretch and somehow find itself again like the skin of a worm might. The images I saw resembled something living almost like sky-bound jellyfish. This movement would alter the craft's exterior and go slightly transparent as it did so. For all I knew, these craft could have been living entities rather than just being piloted by them. Their performances were as angelic and graceful as they were stomach-turning, similar to the way we might observe an assortment of marine life in a stretch of coral. We would be mesmerised and in awe of the colourful selection of tropical fish yet be repulsed by the sudden appearance of an ugly stingray. That mix of feelings were what I had during the dream.

Because the dreams lacked sequence, the implications were a mystery. I did feel however that I had some meaningful communion going on with the scene around me. The entire night sky was lit up with living craft and I doubt that the scene would have limited itself to just my eyes. The whole world would have been able to see what I saw that night in the dream. If there was ever a mass arrival coming from the heavens, that was it!

With all the dreams and heightened strangeness going on in my life at the time added to its fascination and confusion, the next logical step should have been professional investigation. Hypnosis would have been an obvious choice but there was something about this option that just wouldn't give. Maybe that was a mystery in itself, a factor probably owing to my lifelong programming. So much bizarre activity continued that the possibility of hypnosis either got overlooked or just wasn't an issue. There was also my history of pre-conceived beliefs that made this barrier extremely difficult to succumb.

I had always maintained that I could not be hypnotised. This was partly rational and partly pre-conceived. Rational in the sense that I knew myself too well and how I would respond to being induced to a deep and relaxed state. I had always been this hypersensitive individual with a marked inability to keep still and my concentration span could be distracted by the tiniest of turbulence existing outside or in. I always suspected that I suffered from an extreme (non-fearful) nervous disposition or maybe even a level of consciousness so heightened that therapies such as hypnosis would probably seem crude. Simply getting me to relax would have been a challenge.

On the other hand, something inside was manipulating my opinions. It was like having a type of "internal killjoy" that kept strongly dissuading me whenever this impetuousness about approaching someone crept in. Again I would have this mental burning sensation as I approached a taboo area of the Programmer's work. I found this programming to be so clever that it would actually alter my opinions. It would make the exciting prospect of divulging my knowledge appear unappealing. The chances of revealing my experiences to anyone appeared rather slim.

However, this was the stage in life that I was learning how they were not infallible. The recent breakthrough seemed to have made these entities panic, as if a terrible leakage had begun. I honestly felt now that there could be no denying in what was happening, starting with that memory of the school medical room, the psychic experiences and all of the bizarre dreams. The more they struggled to fix the leak the more it would escape in other areas. Their work seemed to be erupting in me prematurely. I was starting to think they were probably right; perhaps I wasn't ready for any of this. It appeared to be more than I could contain.

Their tactics at making me doubt things were indeed powerful and I suspect desperate measures went into that. There were days when I would think all of this was nonsense and just a product of my overactive and dreamy immaturity. I was terribly despondent when this happened. How could I ever put this doubting down to any outside influence? Sometimes I would suspect it was just the disappointing symptoms of a late arrival into adulthood rather than the work of ethereal controllers. Deep down I seemed to know that these "controllers" were actually the string-pullers of my whole belief system.

Some of their induced doubts worked easier than others. The medical room incident, for example could have been an ill-recalled fantasy while the dreams were just dreams. Whenever the other ruminations occurred about paper objects sticking to me, the mutual dreaming or any of the undeniable psychic oddities, something else took place. Amnesia, or at least a botched attempt at it. Strange beings and their abilities to induce amnesia have always been a source of wonder for both UFOlogy and folklore. I have started to see a pattern in this ability. Memories of the obvious psychic incidents were not completely wiped out but instead fabricated with other things. Whenever I tried to recall certain incidents, a haze would wash over, allowing everything to become distorted. The moving objects became manifestations of clumsiness; the mutual dreaming was just the product of something my fiancé and I had previously seen; and the event with the female co-worker who claimed to have psychic abilities was no more than a coincidence. Ingeniously engineered rubbish!

As feeble as these explanations had become and as often as they had failed to convince me, there were times when they would consume me like horrible realisations. There were so many times when I would accept the denial and try to get on with my life. Other times, the reality of the events screamed through and begged for investigation. These were the times that the Programmers seemed to fear most and they were now about to take a further measure to eradicate these ideas indefinitely, even if that meant approaching me in physical form.

If these entities had managed to nest in my mind or have always been there, I was at last developing an intuition to know of their presence and their motives. It was as if this telepathic link I had with them was starting to work both ways, I could now feel their anxiousness, their mutual decisions about what action to take. The time had come where something radical was about to take place, although I couldn't be certain what. I knew from my actions and personal behaviour that something was brewing and I was somehow being prepared for it.

Why had I suddenly taken to isolated places like national parks? I found myself regularly visiting the most remote places and feeling a desire to be far away from crowds, from being visible. This was strange behaviour even for a natural loner because it wasn't the kind of privacy I normally chose. In fact, going to these places didn't feel like a compulsion of my own. I would find myself standing in the middle of a field afterwards wondering why. All I would remember was this strong desire to be away from it all, to become ensconced totally in nature and to enjoy the oneness with everything around me. As much as I appreciated natural beauty, I never really cared for it to the extent of desiring this type of isolation. Something pulled the strings to my new found passions and I was well aware of it. Questioning or arguing with the string pullers was just not a part of the equation; it would be like trying to maintain control within the deepest dream. I would always wonder how long and to what extent this has been going on. Were they the reason for my lifelong tendencies to be a private person? It is said that loneliness is a choice but I am starting to wonder if any of our unexplained tendencies are choices.

Many of my unexplained excursions would often leave me stranded in the middle of a well known local park, a place that I had no idea was significant. Richmond Park is one of our most pleasant and unspoilt nature reserves, and is located around the areas of south west London and Surrey. Because of its vastness, roads are built to allow for traffic and wild deer are free to roam. There are no restrictions on time or boundary in this park which makes it an ideal excursion for families, lovers or anyone just wishing to wander idly. It is a place I frequent from time to time, particularly as I live local but during this period it was somewhere I was becoming magnetically drawn to. I seem to have been attracted to the park's most isolated reaches far away from visitors and would find myself wandering off the pathways and across fields to get there. This would happen either at sunset or night time, usually when crowds were absent.

What I actually did when I arrived there remains a mystery. I remember sitting there enjoying the natural isolation of it all, taking it in and being a part of the tranquillity around me. Watching the sun set behind the trees was part of the passion and seeing its light gradually diminish around me felt like magic. What seems strange is that this scenario would normally have frustrated me no end owing to my usual restlessness and mental over-activity. The relaxed state that normally takes time to acquire seemed to have been with me all of a sudden without really having to apply myself.

In hindsight, I was meditating. Without being in a trance or using any of the concentration techniques, I was as they say "at one with nature", breathing it in and harmonizing with it. This had been happening for days and without warning. If this was an altered state, it would probably explain why I could never fully recall it and why the time appeared to pass so quickly. All I would remember was leaving late at night feeling very refreshed. I was convinced something scientific had taken place rather than natural because these feelings seemed to have been artificially imposed, injected almost. They were however very agreeable and I only wish I could summon them at will.

These lonely excursions had carried through to the autumn of '94. I remembered it being a particularly pleasant summer and feeling for the first time a true inner calm together with a suspicious loss of interest in the Programmers. My newly formed appreciation of nature seemed to have replaced this obsession and I found myself regularly visiting the park to be among the pleasant changes of the season.

There was something else about this period of time that was also out of place involving strange objects or visions. Whenever I was in the Richmond area, I often recalled seeing things from the corner of my eye. Something bright and colourful seemed to flash past me in the night sky but whenever I looked up it was gone. There would also be the total out-of-character tendency for me to ignore it.

There was also something that occurred to me about the phenomena of alien technology and their supposed ability to read minds. If these were the spaceships occasionally reported, they or the pilots must have possessed an uncanny awareness of people witnessing them. I suspected they might have even been playing games with me because I would definitely see an object up there in the sky from my peripheral vision. As I looked towards that something, it would vanish. Could these craft whether living entities or intelligently piloted be accurate enough to read the moment when I looked at them? Could they really manoeuvre or vanish that fast?

There were times when I considered that there were no craft up there at all, just mind games induced by the Programmers which probably explained why I often lost interest. This theory was soon shattered when I actually had witnesses. During this time, I lived in my bachelor flat, and my parents would often come over to visit. Years later they briefly commented about how they would occasionally see a bobbing light in the distance through my kitchen window. This always appeared when we were eating at the table with my back conveniently turned to the window. They claimed not to have mentioned it at the time due to their thinking that it was only a distant plane or something. On one occasion they claimed that it was much closer and thought it was a helicopter looking for something in the area with its full search beam on. When they went home that evening, they discussed why they couldn't hear a propeller going. It was dead silent.

When I speak of mind games, I imagine the Programmers took this a step further by proving they were up in the sky and not just inducing the image. This strikes me how horribly sophisticated their deviance can be. When my parents visited, they knew how to take advantage of the moment without me witnessing them. I think that even if I had a secret camera installed with telescopic lens observing the sky that night, they would have got wind of it. It is certainly a good thing if these beings do have an intellect aimed at responsible behaviour because technology and ESP like that could be unthinkable otherwise. It spooks me to think how this could be used in common espionage, voyeurism even.

Although the sophistication of their technology appears to dwarf ours, I still feel there is fallibility somewhere in the system. I have noticed that whatever they do, it is like a detailed master-plan with very little back up for the unexpected. Stringent calculations and dead reckoning can become quite vulnerable when exposed to spontaneity. The Programmers, not unlike the psychology of our own computer programmers do not like spontaneity. Should you do anything spur of the moment or out of the ordinary without any preconception whatsoever, they would be thrown. Looking back, had I glimpsed this light in the sky, deliberately ignored it and then spun round to view them head on, I would probably have caught them in their process. It seemed that every tendency I had might have been somehow registered with them so that every move becomes predictable. Unfortunately I had no awareness of this flaw at the time.

They obviously make mistakes. This recent leakage of memories was probably caused by spontaneity somewhere and this combined with my stubborn will to remember must have thrown them considerably. I had also sensed their despair over this. Once being plunged into this disarray another stage of the plan would take over. This period of my life was another phase of their master-plan, a phase that was about to end. What I was currently going through with the "night walks" was just part of an ongoing drill for something big about to happen.

One particular evening during that autumn of 1994 I would take my very last night walk. Up until now it had been a regular excursion, at least 3 or

4 times a week. Perhaps the regularity of these visits would pave the way for the big evening in question so that the final journey would not appear too unusual.

That "evening" soon came around. I never did recall the actual date but it was certainly an important event in the Programmer's calendar. Everything about this evening was pre-arranged so that by sunset, I would just get the same compulsion to get up and walk to my nearest rural open space. Nothing would appear strange about this as I had been doing it regularly. Once again, the urge overcame the logic and even while I tried to rationalise, I was putting on my jacket to leave.

It was one of those delightful crisp autumn evenings. I watched a deep orange sun set behind some trees thinking how wholesome everything looked. All around me was a pleasure to take in and that I suspect was intended, a type of acclimatisation with the new state of mind. It wasn't hard for me to break into this new state as I had been doing it often and in all honesty it was tranquil. I must have appeared hypnotised as I walked along that evening, making my way to the park. Not that I noticed many people; I was quite oblivious to anyone around me.

As always I would enter the park by the main gate. As soon as I was in, I would begin on the main path before deviating off to the left. This was strange because it would lead visitors nowhere and was just an empty grazing field for the deer. Still I would carry on walking, adamant about where I was heading. I sometimes wonder if this had ever attracted attention because it would have seemed very odd, a passer-by just walking off into nowhere like that. I can remember wandering towards some shrubs that eventually became bushes and as I waded through these, I would come to a huge grassy opening that was completely out of sight. Years later when my true revelations took place, I would return to this very spot and see what was so unique about it. The only conclusion I could come to was its isolation. I'm not sure if I remembered any birds or animals coming to this part of the park, least of all during nightfall. It was an excellent place to be at one with yourself without disturbance, to perform practices like Tai-Chi or Yoga.

All I remembered doing was sitting there and breathing in the dry air around me. In hindsight I remember feeling relieved that it always rained on the days that I refrained from coming here. That was uncanny. The beings knew the weather forecast so that I wouldn't be sent here those evenings to get soaked? As if the cold rain might upset the trance perhaps? There were some things about this phenomenon that I would never truly get to the bottom of.

This evening was different from the rest. Although I felt at peace, there was a nagging feeling of agitation as if I knew that I wasn't quite alone. This was not a presence of threat, just an odd feeling of being watched. I knew that as I looked upwards, the familiar flash that I had been experiencing would vanish as always. This small light seemed to be behind me and no matter how many times I turned around it always remained that way. The suspicion I had about it tonight was that it was perhaps closer than normal. I could detect its faint glow shining at me from behind, outshining the light from the sunset even. I remember watching my shadow waver whenever it moved and this would go on whatever way I turned.

My feelings tonight were also odd as this presence really didn't scare me. It was as though I had been expecting it or at least prepared to expect it. I thought I'd try to play a game with the object, which seemed to move with my movements. What if I lay on the grass and only moved my eyes? This outcome proved fascinating. I lay down and could still see it there out from the corner of my eye. If I were to tilt my head slightly it would just move accordingly. It reminded me of the games I used to play as a child where I would just lay on my garden lawn and stare up into the blue sky watching thousands of transparent molecules darting around wildly—the cells of my eyeball. I would focus on one and watch it move in accordance with my own eye movement. That's what it was like watching this thing. I have come to suspect that an advanced race of beings perhaps use a type of remote spying device that is so sharp it can monitor you while staying outside of your line of vision.

Now that it was getting darker, I noticed another ingenious facet of this monitor. The device got lighter as the night become darker. I was now seeing a more pronounced image of the device from my peripheral vision as it began to shine. I could now see that there were more than one and they had all been around me like hovering blind spots. I would have estimated there were about seven, spheres no bigger than a golf ball. I could never see this many during the day and couldn't get over how quickly they moved. The nearest thing I could equate them to were the stars sometimes seen after receiving a knock. I was quite literally seeing stars, golden flashes whizzing around just outside my vision as if I had suddenly been hit. What did any of this mean?

I stood back up and began walking. The flashes were not so apparent. I felt uncomfortable at the bright appearance of these things and their sudden number. Still noticing them slightly from the corner of my eye, I walked around and observed what was around me. Night had fallen quickly with the sky becoming that inky blue giving way to occasional patches of light blue. It was deathly silent with hardly any wind to be heard even through the collection of dried leaves. It didn't feel natural tonight and I still harboured that feeling of being watched.

Now that it was dark, the balls of light were accompanied by their reflections on the floor, which were quick and hard to follow. It seemed as if I was being followed by fireflies which couldn't be properly seen.

Without any direction and hardly any night vision, I paced around in circles. I could just make out the outline of trees and bushes in the distance. There was something else in the corner of my eye that appeared much slower than the fireflies and to my amazement didn't divert when my eyes turned to meet it. What I saw was a dimly lit crescent shape in the distance just shimmering there in the sky.

Whatever it was, it made no sound and remained stationary. Something else was out of character with me tonight, my emotions. That was clearly a UFO up there in the sky. Not just a disappointing weather balloon but an actual unidentified flying object spotted for the first time. Why wasn't I jumping with anticipation and my excitement uncontrollable over this lifelong interest that was finally revealing itself to me that night? The Programmers held the reins again, restraining my emotions and making the scene appear like a dream.

One faculty that they did allow me tonight was at least some of my awareness. I clearly knew that the craft up there was unclassified and simply shouldn't have been there. It didn't resemble any craft flown by the British military and had no place in our flying zones. It couldn't have been mistaken for the "helicopter" my parents claimed to have seen that night or resemble anything my naked eyes were used to seeing.

The craft was alien and my knowledge of that didn't cause a stir. I remember the outline or shape of the craft being similar to a boomerang although shorter and more compact. Its colours pulsated and changed, white and then yellow, mutating into a brilliant red and finally to a rich green. This colour sequence repeated whilst the craft remained there engulfed in a hazy mist.

Probably the most memorable thing about this sighting was that the object's light was not particularly bright, yet it was a painful effort to look directly at it. It should have been no more intense to the eye than a distant night view of traffic lights but it felt like a spotlight being shone straight at me. I could only look directly at it in brief periods, similar to the way you might try to look at the sun on the horizon.

One thing occurred to me about this object: it was also aware of me. This probably justified my feelings of being watched. Whether this was a living thing or it had a pilot, it knew I was there and it could have homed right in on my mind. In fact, that was the other aspect I felt when looking up at this strange body, what if a particular communion was going on, the same type I had experienced with nature recently? I noticed I was losing track of everything else around me, the fireflies were gone and so was the oneness I felt with the environment. So many external factors had been blocked out. The presence of this craft caused a thick atmosphere as if the scene had moved under water.

I kept looking away due to the unexplainable ferocity of the craft's light but fascination insisted I keep glancing back much to the strain of my eyes. I couldn't keep still and had to move around. Even the sound of my footsteps indicated something very wrong. The expected sound of dried leaves being crushed underfoot sounded as though it was coming from a distance just like being under water. Something was also terribly strange about the scene around me; sounds were suffocating and the appearance of things in the distance was becoming faint, lightening even. The vague outline of trees and bushes were no longer visible as everything had taken the appearance of whiteness. I suddenly began to understand that I had plunged into a new universe where the only two bodies existing were me and the craft. All else was devoid.

The strange whiteness seemed to have replaced the night and all else visible within it. All activity around me had been absorbed into an eerie silence. Perhaps this was another unexplored state of the Oz Factor, a strange white realm with drowned out sounds and a sensation of moving through syrup. As I tried to move, I remembered that feeling of sluggishness where everything resembled slow motion as if the white fabric around me had an unaccounted denseness. Even at the time it occurred to me how similar it was to those dreams where you would be stuck to the spot and a train would be coming towards you and no matter how hard you tried to move, your muscles would simply not respond or would be exceptionally slow in doing so.

Through the whiteness, the craft was still visible with its faint glow that continued to hurt my eyes. I couldn't attribute this bizarre replacement of the night to light from the craft; it didn't appear to be the source of the whiteness. It continued to pulsate the same sequence of colours, yet white was the colour engulfing everything.

I don't remember this thing ever moving, yet it appeared to be much nearer now, which could have been just a trick owing to the absence of everything. Its only movement was the pulsating motion and mutation of colours which mesmerised me to the point of ignoring any other movement it might have made. Equally fascinating was its silence and I wonder if the imagery alone was a factor making me imagine sound or if there was something else communicative going on. With this silence and what I already know about the Oz Factor, a kind of communion could indeed have happened although I'm not sure how. It was very much the "oneness" I felt earlier about nature rather than actual messages being transmitted. Now it was just this thing and I and perhaps that alone was significant.

I remembered it making me feel docile and pliable for whatever was on the agenda. This docility came over me in extreme tiredness. My eyes began to burn and my legs turned to jelly. I became over-ridden with the sensation of wanting to lie down and ignore everything for a few minutes and recalled thinking how strange this must have looked. I was in a public place being summoned by a huge floating cell, a scene that could have been apparent from miles away yet not a soul was present. My only feelings were of retreat, wanting to lie down in a nearby bush or something.

I needed to at least sit if not lie down. I was no longer aware of any shrubs or soft patches of grass because I could see nothing but a white haze. Walking away in any direction was difficult as there was no longer an East or West and the sensation would be like wading against a tide. I just felt the need to crouch to ease the fatigue in my lower back and legs. As

I did I reached down with both hands to touch the floor and to my relief felt the cool dry grass beneath me. I couldn't actually see it, just the dense consistency of the whiteness everywhere but I at least knew I was still in the park.

That was it. I could finally crouch down onto the grass and roll onto my side. It was a good sensation and I felt at peace though I knew this oddity still hovered above. Perhaps acting submissive and ignoring it might cause it ignore me, like playing possum.

None of this would have been the rational action to take in circumstances like these, but in the unexplored territory of the Otherness the dream logic rule.

This thing wanted me sleepy and unquestioning and that was the way it would be. I closed my eyes tightly and covered my head with my arms to block out the persistent white.

Losing consciousness was incredibly easy that night and it was the last I remembered.

3

Activation

My nose was cold and blocked with dry lips from breathing only through my mouth. This and the cold air against my face brought me nearer to the surface. I could also detect a pleasant morning sun and heard birds singing.

Wherever I was or whatever had happened, I was fully clothed and in a particularly uncomfortable position. The occurrences of last night had left me lying crouched here on the grass, sheltering from chill, and by morning I would be astonished as to how I actually slept this way.

My bones killed me as I moved myself to come around and everything ached when I tried to collect each stiff limb. I stood up and stretched, hearing every bone crack which felt oddly pleasant. My bleary eyes acclimatised to the fresh morning sun and misty field around me and I remembered feeling collected enough to enjoy coming around unrushed.

Remembering the previous night wasn't as easy. A huge question mark would hang over everything as I tried to remember it, which was why I didn't bother. I knew how things were out of place ranging from why I spent so long watching the sun set to the way someone like myself with irrationally stringent sleep requirements could crash out so easily, like an old vagabond. Trying to account for things would make my head burn in the usual way so I just shelved these confusions for later and enjoyed the morning.

I noticed how different this field was during his time of day to the way it was when I visited it during my strange evening trips. Rather than taking in the natural serenity and silence that I enjoyed at sunset, it seemed to offer more activity during the day. For the first time, I noticed deer grazing in the distance and other wildlife. I heard birds singing, which was strangely absent when I came here at night. If I stretched my eyes that bit further, I would see people, joggers and other folk taking the scenic route to work.

It must have been around 8.30 and I was in no hurry to report into work. I was, after all, a contractor too small and superfluous to really be missed. Numbers in the workplace these days seemed to have long replaced the acknowledgement of individuals.

Had I died in this park last night, I wonder how long it would have taken for the authorities to identify my corpse? I often wonder this when taking into account the untold vagrants that are seen wandering aimlessly and seem unaccounted for. When they are found dead, it only becomes a tiny statistic.

Who, for instance, would have been aware of my manoeuvres over the past couple of weeks when mysteriously visiting this park during odd hours? I hadn't been committing an offence and would have no reason to be followed but had something happened (UFO abduction), could it ever be accounted for? If the abduction phenomenon exists then I suspect that our increased sense of freedom and autonomy over the years has offered abductors the ideal climate for their manoeuvres. Nobody knew or cared that I was here and my obsession for privacy had insisted this. It all seemed to be engineered perfectly. At the end of the day the finger of suspicion could point at nobody but me.

If something strange did happen last night, there would certainly have been no witnesses, not even a deer. The only sense I ever have of being watched is by the beings themselves that I term the Programmers. Not only did these beings observe my actions, they observed and altered my thoughts.

My knowledge of last night could well have been altered. The likelihood of me spending the night here was pretty remote. I still possessed the faculty of curiosity but didn't remember being too perturbed by the event upon waking. I seemed more concerned with my basic needs; I just wanted a hot coffee and the chance to properly collect myself.

I strolled across fields, intending to find the nearest pathway. I was clearly off the beaten track. I remembered trudging through high grass and reeds wondering why on earth I would have come out this far. All I could recollect was the desire to be alone although this would not explain how

I instinctively knew where to go. I could not have found a more isolated spot in the park unless given a map and I had no prior knowledge of the whereabouts apart from the obvious tourist areas.

I could at last see hints of the civilised world that I hid from last night. The first activity I saw were dogs being exercised in the distance, an appeasing picture of domestic life that I seemed to welcome that morning. Further on I would see joggers and families all going about their business, totally remote to my evening of strangeness.

Through the overgrown shrubs I could at last see a path leading me to somewhere that I might recognise. I carried on and made out through sleepy eyes an area of familiarity. If I was right, this section of the park would lead me to a nearby clearing where cars park and a local lodge could be found. This was where strollers would find toilets and a pleasant refreshments pantry. The desired coffee wouldn't be far away.

I managed to find myself a seat that pleasantly caught the morning sun and enjoyed one cup after another. Something had seriously drained me in the recent hours, and I required more recuperation than normal. Surprisingly the unknown events of the previous night seemed to become a chore to try to recall and I couldn't think why. I had been doing things very out of character the past few weeks and last night couldn't have been stranger. My usual sleep problems would make sleeping in a luxury hotel difficult and the idea of roughing it seemed absurd. All I could recall was the sudden fatigue and a series of ludicrous dreams thereafter. The dreams didn't seem as important as my purpose for coming to the park, particularly last night. I suspected that I wasn't alone during those hours but that was just another odd notion that I couldn't justify.

Coming around was easy. I snuggled into my warm bomber jacket sipping coffee as I watched the world go by. I might have been just another wandering drunk who spent the night in the park. As always there was never a shred of evidence the next day to support the suspicions, just vague memories of a non-addressed oddity. No conclusion had been met and no confusion was solved. I remembered feeling disappointed at this stage because something prevented me from remembering. Last night's sunset was an effort to process and trying to recall what happened afterwards was impossible. My efforts were met with the familiar burning sensations as I tried to cross that mental boundary.

I seemed to harbour another disappointing feeling, one that I'm sure was instigated by the Programmers, and that was doubt. What if nothing at all had taken place last night? What if it was just another of those weird phases, only this time you fell asleep? I knew these impressions weren't justified but as there was nothing else, they had substance.

As I left the park that morning, it was the start of a new phase in my life, a very sober and cynical one. However, the evidence from my past that suggested strange things going on seemed to keep this wavering door open. In other words there were times when I just felt agnostic. Belief would be met "if" there was supporting evidence but other than that, I would just put my experiences down to partially remembered dreams. No longer would I become preoccupied with "fantasy'. Whatever the Programmers were trying to achieve was in some ways working out as I was quickly losing interest in the encounters. In fact, I was embarrassed to admit having them.

As always, there were conflicts going on in my mind. The believer would challenge the cynic. During this period, the cynic nearly always outweighed the believer. Only supportive evidence could arm the believer, but that was never easy to come by.

However, I later experienced something that was near to physical evidence. I was suffering a burning sensation in my eyes ever since that night in the park. Quite often they would stream and sting slightly during the day where I found myself rapidly blinking for relief. I could only put this down to the time I watched the sun go down in the park and couldn't honestly think of anything any other cause.

I went to see a doctor regarding my eyes. He shattered any hopes I had of recovering strange memories.

"What do you expect if you gaze at the sun with a naked eye?" he said, harrumphing.

Not that I would have dreamed of mentioning UFOs, but he had done the Programmers a huge favour by making that diagnosis. It reassured me that nothing happened. I certainly wasn't going to mention the strange dreams either, the ones that I was convinced related to my affected eyes. All I could do was grudgingly agree how silly it was to look at the sun, even when setting.

To my knowledge, this is the only physical complaint ever experienced from encounters. Although I do recall episodes in my life when dreams would leave odd physical traces. I remember certain dreams of walking barefoot through rocky, volcanic terrains and only upon recall of the dreams did my feet actually start to hurt. I would astonishingly find blisters on my soles the following morning. This is not an unusual phenomena and not necessarily paranormal. There has been much research into the "mind over matter" theory where people suffering from psychosomatic tendencies report physical changes influenced by thought. Thinking of aches and pains can sometimes make them manifest and even imagining illness has been known to cause them. This same trigger of thought proved to be trick with my sore eyes. I went away convinced that it was the sun, but strangely my eyes only started to hurt when I recalled a particular dream. A dream I had about a UFO that same night in the park. The one I remember that made my eyes squint with discomfort was in a very abstract way, one of a pulsating and colourful craft.

I dreamt that the early evening sky had come alive and was watching me from above. A particular section of the sky seemed nearer and became fluid in appearance. When I looked at it closely I realised this patch was a different colour from the rest and its fluidness allowed it to change colour. I began to realise that what I was looking at was a bubble shape with a faint luminance that shouldn't have hurt my eyes to look at yet it did. There were a few colours being displayed up there but whenever red came into focus it hurt and even thinking about it seems to strike my retina. I don't remember a real sequence to the dream, but the UFO part was what my eyes fiercely responded to.

Looking back, I wouldn't have glared at a sunset for long periods, as I am only too aware of the dangers. But it would amaze me how a dream, even for a psychosomatic person (which I'm not) can cause physical damage. No dream can conjure up UV light, for instance yet the doctor who inspected both my retinas insisted it was just that.

Whatever suspicion it had left me with, I couldn't account for it, so I settled for the easier option of the cynic. I felt foolish and disappointed and just wanted to get on with my life. My intrigue with UFOs and the paranormal wasn't as easy to extinguish. I still wanted to read up on these subjects but found it so much easier to treat as something that happens to others. On a personal level, I remained indifferent.

The case was closed. These Programmer beings had successfully managed to install a mechanism that would first lead me to disappointment and then cynicism. The programme appeared to do exactly as it was intended. Whenever my mind approached that boundary of suspicion, I would first feel this self-deceit followed by an overwhelming doubt as to why anyone would believe these things happened to them. This was a radical change from the person I was before the nightly excursions to the park.

Even today I feel perturbed by their capabilities of mind control. It makes human attempts at this seem rather crude by comparison. I refer to our stage hypnotists who can make subjects act out any part they wish just by the power of suggestion yet they insist that the subject's "core self" cannot be altered. They cannot make the person go out and murder if it isn't within their fundamental persona. I honestly feel that alien beings can go steps ahead of this and re-write someone's core self if they wished. Judging by my own shift in beliefs since that night in the park, I suspect I was going through that.

Things that I would naturally avoid I suddenly became open to regardless of any prejudices that had steered me away in the past. The main change in me was study, a discipline I had avoided like the plague after academic failure at school.

Science was one of the natural interests I always had but that normally stretched no further than the theories behind my favourite sci-fi. But that was changing. I now found myself visiting libraries and losing myself for hours in those huge stuffy textbooks that I avoided at school. All of a sudden I found myself meticulously combing the shelves for Einstein or anything to do with quantum physics, atomic science or the metaphysical. It's true that I always had an interest in these things but now I was looking at the hows and whys behind them and also managing the concentration threshold that I never thought possible. It was great to be able to digest things this way without drifting off on a useless tangent.

The way I grasped and retained the information I read brought me to another conclusion—that perhaps my intelligence was extending. Perhaps it would no longer be restricted the way I felt it had been before. The best move I considered was to seize the momentous breakthrough by embarking on full time education and accelerate from wherever it was I floundered before.

My current job appeared to be needing me less and less and it would only be a matter of time before redundancy reared its ugly head. Being a contractor, this meant no pay so I wasn't going to wait around for the wounding. I handed in my month's notice and used this time to browse course literature while applying for a student grant. I had no particular career aims in mind other than knowing I wasn't going to fulfil my childhood dream of becoming a stage magician. All I wanted to do for now was engulf myself with the subject that always fascinated me, science.

I immediately enrolled at a local college for a science degree, pretending that I already had the formal entry qualifications. When I began the course I was rather dubious about that reckless decision thinking it would leave me mercilessly slacking behind. At first there were signs of this but my new thirst for knowledge soon helped me catch up on my peers without any painful effort. After all, what I lacked were the foundations, the facts and figures that enabled my fellow students to sail through but these were soon acquired by the way I had applied myself. Something had definitely happened in the way I developed this new ability to concentrate and grasp things. Normally the sheer capabilities of the students around me would have discouraged me no end, yet I went into this course like a hungry man wanting information about the world around me. It seemed that any doubts or disadvantages were just secondary to this odd enthusiasm.

Both mentally and socially, unexplained steps had been taken. For the first time I was taking a broader interest in the world rather than just my obsessive interests. I had made friends amongst peers and gathered a small circle of people with mutual interests. We shared a particular interest in conventional science and where it borders with the unknown. During breaks I would regularly engage with students about these subjects and how they touch upon areas that little is known about. How far can you break down atoms? Could they ever be magnified to the infinitely small where they perhaps exist as microscopic planets, populated by micro-entities?

Naturally these interests would spread into areas such as the existence of God, the afterlife and higher species of life in the cosmos. During tea breaks, these subjects would be discussed fervently and I certainly surprised myself just how much I had to contribute. So many students seemed to have at least a passing interest in these matters and would occasionally join in the discussions but there would always be this "hardcore" of the liaisons consisting of just three—myself and another couple who I will call Paul and Wendy. It turned out that Paul and Wendy, a married couple from the Southwest coast were both members of a UFO organisation who attended conferences across the country. I expressed my own interest in these things without giving away any suspicion I had about possibly being involved (taking into account that suspicion was rapidly fading.)

Paul and Wendy shared the same agnostic approach to the subject that I had recently developed, applying healthy scepticism where it was needed. None of us confessed to ever having unusual experiences ourselves but maintained that unwavering fascination in all things esoteric. Something was already forming in this relationship that would prove to be the seeds of a new organisation with new objectives to the world of the paranormal. What we all had in our approaches, particularly with UFOlogy was a hard-nosed "straight to the jugular" belief that wouldn't waste time with sightings or disputable factors but focus more on the closer encounters and first hand accounts. In other words we spent very little time discussing the arguable hard evidence that initially come with these phenomena and homed in right on stories of alleged meetings with extraterrestrials and where ghosts really come from. For instance, it wasn't enough that we might meet someone who claims to have seen a ghost, we wanted to know what the ghost had to say! Was it a conscious communicative entity or a manifestation of a possible time warp?

We became a trio, mutually aware that something was going to grow from our relationship. So many nights after college we would continue our discussions in local pubs and in each other's houses. I became a member of their nationwide UFO organisation and attended many conferences across the country. People were starting to think of us as related at college as we had become a type of clique threesome always engaged in something. That oddity went no further than pure mutual interests. Fate perhaps brought us together and the threesome would inevitably form a legitimate study group.

What we were becoming concerned with was the lack of depth investigating UFO's and why nothing seemed to be followed up. So many stories would be written about sightings and sometimes encounters but what ever happened to the people afterwards? Did they all simply re-emerge into the lives of Mr & Mrs Average? It seemed that the areas we studied were what people really wanted insight to. Everyone read about sightings, made opinions about photographs seen and stories of leaked government documents but what people ultimately wanted to know was "who is actually piloting these things and why are they here?" This appeared to be the gap that we as a small group wanted to fill.

It was mid 1995 and this was a very stimulating period for paranormal subjects. The controversial footage of the Roswell alien autopsy was shown to the public for the first time and that opened a large can of worms. There were also a whole range of UFO and paranormal magazines around at the time, I would estimate about 8 different titles appearing in newsagents. Only one of those magazines is still in circulation.

Naturally this was a good time to take advantage of this public interest and advertise our own proposed study group in one of those magazines. We as a threesome knew what our objectives would be from the extensive conversations we had and what we needed was a name to spearhead those objectives. This was a tricky point to agree on as the name had to conjure up what we were all about and what would set us aside from the other research groups listed. In a nutshell, we wanted to be the study that dealt with "closer encounters" so Paul decided this should inevitably be the name. I was uncomfortable with Closer Encounters, likening it to a name given to contact services for explicit affairs rather than a serious study group. My idea for a fitting name would be CE5 as we would be specialising in the next progressive step from the phenomena of CE4—the level of contact involving abduction. CE5 (close encounter of the 5th kind) would explain our research accurately, the phase of contact addressing communication and the final phase of interaction.

We agreed that it wasn't necessarily the most original title and suspected that someone somewhere might just be using it. After scanning the latest copies of all the current publications on the subject, it appeared that nobody had claimed "CE5" so fortunately it was ours.

Wendy had set up a mailing address with the local Post Office for anyone interested as we weren't confident enough at this stage to deal with personal enquiries. I had managed to word and print up some useful group literature using a local library's PC and Paul combed the area for possible meeting places in the future. Luckily he was blessed verbally and was appointed "group leader" to introduce and co-ordinate these future gatherings and explain our study to people.

My job would be to deal with the group's literature such as postal enquiries and future club newsletters which at first I didn't think would generate much interest. To my surprise, when the advert had finally gone out to one of the magazines, we received a bigger response rate than imagined. People were certainly curious about these subjects at the time and whatever was spreading through the public interest opened up a whole new door for us.

At first we were nervous by the rate of response, particularly as a new group taking on paranormal research. On reflection I would say that 60% of the enquirers were just curious and once I mailed their information, they would no doubt shelve it for another day. That was fine; the least it would do was perhaps generate news of our group. The 40% that did pursue it replied almost immediately and seemed adamant to meet up and start chasing flying saucers. It would then be up to us, the threesome to arrange a meeting for hungry enquirers and make our aims clear to them right away. I think that most of them were unaware that we were a brand new organisation with a membership of just three. There seemed to be all kinds of expectations during the time and in hindsight I can understand why.

People in general want things tailor made and normally when approaching an organisation like us, they hope it will be an established group. Deep down they were hoping, as I would have if approaching a study group, to find a resourceful niche that will confirm that the unexplained is real. We needed them for contribution as much as they needed us for addressing their needs and interests. At the end of the day we could not produce a spaceship or provide true grounding for their beliefs.

Personally, I wanted to emphasise some scepticism to the study because that was largely how I had been feeling then. It wasn't because I wanted to shatter any hopes or impose opinions, it's just that I had tasted so much disappointment that I didn't want to lead anyone else up this path. The objective of the group was, after all, closer encounters, to concentrate on the nucleus of the phenomena while cutting away sightings, commentaries and so on. We would look at two possibilities—these things either existed or they didn't. CE5 were open to both suggestions but aimed to work on the former.

Our 40% was still a considerably large response and Paul had arranged a first seminar/meeting in a local community hall. It wasn't the favoured choice as we had originally hoped for a hotel conference room but due to our tiny budget, we would make the most with this old council run school hall.

The first meeting was a definite success due to so much nervous preparation by the three of us. Paul, Wendy and I took turns in speaking to welcome the guests, each equipped with an itinerary of what to expect. The initial unease of the first meeting was made easier by the total attentiveness of our guests who surprisingly took in with interest everything we presented without so much as a heckle. Questions were allowed at the end of the session and there were a lot of them. The guests appeared to be a pleasantly mixed bunch with a mixture of input. As expected, the majority wanted to know of forthcoming field events and what they might hope to see on them. This was open to suggestion and would be welcomed with any feedback or ideas even if that meant spending a night in a haunted castle. We were set up as a research group that wanted to get closer. I was willing to go the distance with that side of the research and would personally find it an enlightening challenge.

Quite a few people wanted to know of useful reading on the subjects such as book reviews and there were others who sought the hobbyist aspects, looking to collect information, group literature and so forth. A cross-section of enquirers with a mixture of input but overall it was a success. The ages ranged also from the teens to twenties (many who wanted sky watching trips that turned into outdoor parties) to the middle-aged with a marked and surprising interest in the paranormal.

Over the coming months there would be subsequent meetings but as expected, less attendance than the first due to the many "samplers." It was interesting to see the same faces as these would turn out to be the new core of our future membership. Both Paul and Wendy felt confident enough to supply their phone number to new and prospective members. A small but reputable research group was now forming and things looked promising for CE5.

Despite all the developments in my life, I still felt the need to reserve special times for myself. Maybe I could appreciate these moments more now that I had all the necessary human distractions during the day. Apart from the study which was becoming surprisingly rewarding, I still seemed to need that special time with my thoughts, something I would cherish. Aside from the recent "belief shift" that had transformed me into someone more sceptical, there was another side of me that refused to be explored. This seemed to be the special compartment of my mind that the Programmers had for themselves, one which they had allocated for their mechanisms. Tampering with that compartment was a taboo and even sparing curiosity over it was difficult.

Something was to take place in following weeks that made me realise this strangeness wasn't just within. When I think back to this incident I realise that the manipulative power possessed by these beings doesn't just limit itself to the mind. If they want something to happen, they can make it so, anywhere in the world. This happened in the form of a phone call one night by someone who simply identified himself as "Gideon."

Gideon was enquiring about CE5, saying he had seen our ad listed in the magazine. When I asked how he got my number he just said he saw it listed, which I knew was impossible. The only form of contact the advert displayed was a box number and from there on, the only telephone number given out to enquirers would have been Paul and Wendy's. I later checked this with them and they swore they hadn't given my number to anyone. The magazine with CE5's listing didn't even have my number.

He sounded soft-spoken and pleasant enough, and just wanting to know where our next meeting would be. I gave him the details of this without any suspicion, thinking that the business about my number was just a small mishap somewhere. After all, how else could he have obtained it? When I asked if he would like some group literature, such as a newsletter, he declined, saying he would happily collect that at our next gathering. He closed the conversation by asking me if I would like to speak with him when the meeting was over, which I couldn't see any harm in. I thought no more about this until the next meeting was due.

In this time, I assured myself that either Paul or Wendy must have given out my number out in error and then embarrassingly denied it. It didn't really matter, but I hadn't lived at my rented accommodation long, wasn't in the phone book and my social influence certainly didn't stretch far. Locating me by any means couldn't have been easy so it left a question mark. Had I not have liked the sound of whoever he was on the phone, I would probably have told him the group was defunct.

During the next meeting, it was my turn to get up and speak regarding a book review. As I spoke and addressed the audience of about 20, I noticed a face in the crowd that struck me as familiar. A fellow in his early sixties sat on the end of the second row from the back nearest to the radiator whom I seemed to know from somewhere. While you're speaking, it's best not to try to recollect someone in the crowd as it immediately distracts, but this curiosity screamed at me. I carried on my talk, focusing my eyes on nothing but what I was doing. The talk would not be a long one and I would soon be able to go over and meet this person.

Wendy had taken over and presented a slide show, which unfortunately meant the lights were to be dimmed and prevented me from properly seeing this man. I managed to glance over and see as much as I needed to. He was smartly dressed and not unlike anyone else of his age group with grey wispy hair brushed back from a receding line and an interesting moon-shaped face. If he had known me the way I suspected I knew him, he didn't seem to show it as he just sat happily watching what was being presented.

Perhaps the strangest thing was this gut feeling I had that he was the man on the phone. As soon as the presentation ended I went over to introduce myself and, lo and behold, he was the mysterious enquirer calling himself "Gideon." After the formalities, I asked about his name, inquiring whether he was Jewish. He claimed he wasn't but came from a religious family with a tradition of Biblical names. Given the knowledge I now have of this man's covert involvement with my life, I doubt that Gideon was his real name at all. It rang no bells whatsoever as he gave it over the phone apart from my awareness of the Gideon's Bible. It does strike me as interesting however that this name features in the Bible as someone who received a message from a Heavenly angel carrying a fire-emitting staff similar to a magic wand that performed awesome feats. Considering my own obsession with wand-waving magicians and extraterrestrials who do similar things, he seemed to have chosen a catchy name, one which I would investigate years later. As we spoke more about ourselves, it turned out that he had a lifelong interest in the occult and was obviously well read on the subject. I found it strange how blasé he was about these things, as though they were common facts of life.

I had to ask him if I knew him from somewhere and the response was negative. Again there was this impartial brushing aside as though it either wasn't important or he was trying to hide something. This was obviously his first meeting with CE5 and I was sure I hadn't seen him from anywhere I had worked. As we spoke, I could feel a useful friendship forming that would take precedence over any suspicion.

I didn't hesitate in introducing him to the other two founders, but he appeared to have more of a leaning towards me. This would be the start of a strange liaison that at times appeared to be one sided because there was so much he wouldn't disclose, but I didn't feel like probing. Although he certainly demonstrated an interest in my affairs, which I found strange considering our age difference. It wasn't so much my thoughts and feelings that interested him, it was more a case of why. Why do you have a certain opinion and what brought you to that conclusion? appeared to be his angle.

Finally when I asked if he would like to get on our regular mailing list, he declined, insisting that he could pick this information up at meetings. Again there was that avoidance over his address, and I only gleaned that he lived local after he'd given a rough idea of where he would be travelling from. We just left it agreeing to see each other at the next CE5 event and his position remained one of "I'll call you." As we departed in the car park, watching the old man cross the road and disappear into the night, the three of us remained quizzical as to where he was ever coming from. We drove home that night in Paul's car each discussing our surmises as to whether his strangeness pointed to age, paranoia or just the eccentricity that sometimes comes with the esoteric territory.

In the back of our minds we suspected that we had seen the last of the elusive Gideon as many eccentrics have been known to lose interest before moving onto a new subject. On the contrary, he had become our most consistent guest and would arrive at every venue 20 minutes beforehand. The strange thing was that his interest in the group still seemed to have focused upon me. That wasn't to say he was interested in me personally, it was more to do with what I had to say on the subject that kept him enthralled. I continued to find this unusual with our generation gap and particularly when there were a range of books already the subject written by experts older and wiser, most of which he claimed to have read.

The absurdity of this relationship was that he and his angle were as equally fascinating to me. It had reached the point of suspicion where I thought he might have been a type of envoy from a government organisation sent to investigate UFO study groups, but then what was so suspicious about our newly formed little club and why focus on me? This suspicion alone was drawing me towards him in a big way but then there were other attributes to this man that drew attention. Apart from his mysteriousness, he appeared unusually intelligent and interesting to listen to. If this was a form of espionage to form a close relationship, it was working.

Listening to him was never a chore. His articulation of stories became mesmerising and it was hard not to feel magnetised to what he had to say. There was something unusual about his appearance. Although his face was fitting enough for someone of his age, his eyes were something quite different, alien almost. They were large, sombre and seemingly fitting for an oval face but they emitted something vibrant from the pale blue irises like a hypnotic grip. Looking into them seemed to cast a spell yet you remained deeply inquisitive. Whatever that spell was, it was hard to describe. I had always put it down to the enthralling conversation that jelled our relationship but it seemed right from the beginning that peculiar undercurrents were present. Our shared interests sustained the conversations and whatever I brought up he would have a profound knowledge of. Even my obscure interests, the ones I could never account for seemed to be verified through his odd knowledge of things and that interested me no end.

One evening after a CE5 gathering we stayed behind to continue our conversations which I had now come to look forward to. I felt that I knew him well enough to share my disjointed tales of monk magicians who I believed belonged to Masonic covens. Instead of balking at my theories or seeming puzzled, he assured me that what I was referring to was a secretive coven of nature spirits known as Elementals. These were, he said, a common phenomenon of harmless but highly evolved woodland entities who existed as an earth-bound continuation of ancient Wicca people. As my own unexplained knowledge already confirmed, they appeared as hooded beings in brown robes that possessed fantastical feats of power like walking through walls. Gideon went on to tell me how these beings sometimes appeared with "red eyes." I wasn't familiar with that particular aspect but it did strike me as odd how he managed to address so many of my concerns with such accuracy. How did he know these things and what were his own experiences?

Inevitably we went on to talk about another interest of mine, which I was convinced had something to do with my own covert past—freemasons and secret societies. We would talk for hours about ancient Masonic covens, conspiracy theory surrounding the Old Testament, and legends of the ancient scrolls. This led on to the topic of covert masons existing today. As we delved further into the subject he eventually declared that he was a member of such a society. This announcement caused an expected reaction with me and when I look back to the conversation, I realise it was an obvious ploy to lure me. At the time his intentions could not have seemed further away. I instantly became the wide-eyed enthusiast wanting to come along to one of his meetings while he remained the dismissive older patron who advised me otherwise. Forces were at work here as they were from day one when I met this old gentleman. All along he seemed to emit this non-intrusive manipulation of the mind which I'm convinced was more than this intelligence he seemed to possess or just power of suggestion. It was a kind of subtle telepathy, a type that I had come across before that wasn't easy to detect. A telepathy that focused more on emotions and interests than direct communicative thought. He appeared to have the talent to subliminally encourage something while acting out something quite opposite. This seemingly ancient talent stretched further than any common gift of gab.

Forces were undoubtedly at work because I was almost begging him to invite me along to one of his Masonic meetings. I remembered being astonished by my enthusiasm and surprised by what was coming out of my own mouth. His responses would be "why are you so keen? Do you understand what my sect is really about?" Oddly enough I already did without actually asking.

I seemed to know that his society was also a continued generation of an ancient order dating back to I don't know when. Its regular gatherings were based upon ancient ceremonies similar to Wicca. Perhaps an earlier conversation had influenced this sudden burst of knowledge but it wouldn't explain my intuitive certainty. To this day I don't have a name for his mysterious coven, yet I was hell-bent on attending.

I remember his final words that evening being something to the effect of "well, we'll have to see." I got the impression that being accepted into his fold wasn't out of the question but something needing preparation. We parted that night agreeing upon some eventual "initiation" that would take place when I was "ready."

That night had been one of the strangest nights I can remember and appeared to be a radical turning point in my life. I don't know how long I had been speaking with Gideon but it must have been one of my longest and deepest conversations. I wouldn't rule out the possibility of "missing time" because huge chunks of what was said that night eluded me. Missing time seemed to play its part from that night onwards because I don't recall much about the odd period that would follow.

The strange liaison had heralded an even stranger period ahead. I recall the next few months as being a type of automated daze where I just went through the motions of life like a robot. I seemed to suffer patches of amnesia where I wouldn't to remember certain events. It wasn't so much the events themselves that I struggled to remember, it was the "why's" and "how's" behind them. I seemed to be doing things ritually without question. The regular evening visits to secluded places such as the park had continued and I often remember looking forward to these times. As the sun would set I felt a buzz of excitement coming on as though I would be off on a mysterious journey somewhere to meet special people. Consciously, I can only remember these journeys being solitary.

Life didn't appear to taking its usual toll during these months. I seemed to be enjoying a peaceful acceptance of life where I just took things as they came without question or criticism. I again need to refer to my comparisons to the dream state or Oz Factor because the inconsistencies of a dream were all there. I accepted the outrageous and don't remember much about it. Whatever state had been induced, I don't recall it interfering with my daily activities. If anything, it allowed me to sail through them with less stress than I would normally encounter.

My studies were not a problem and never neglected regardless of any oddities going on. Ever since I decided to take on full time study with this science degree, I enjoyed a whole new capacity of accelerated learning. The daily attendance of college and hours of study were a pleasure rather than a chore and I was keeping abreast of my course work despite my lack of academic foundation. The transformation from the boy who didn't even manage a CSE was in contrast a phenomenon!

Even outside study I would read exuberantly from subjects ranging from science to religion and sometimes try to rewrite extracts from the Bible in the way I interpreted them. My fascination with the paranormal was as unrelenting as ever and I seemed to be outgrowing that sceptical patch I had been going through (the induced scepticism, I strongly suspect.)

My activities with CE5 had continued, although I felt there was deterioration in the group due to a lull in the interest from members. The meetings would continue and topics would still be covered but nothing seemed to go any further and that discouraged people. As agreed from the beginning, we could not produce the proverbial spaceship out of the blue which of course meant that CE5 would not live up to its name by accomplishing these things. We would become another study/research group listed in the classifieds of a paranormal magazine and not necessarily make the groundbreaking discoveries that each of us hoped.

My co-founders Paul and Wendy would be expecting their first child very soon and would have greater priorities than the group meetings. Eventually I would see less and less of their company. There were a few others that I had hoped would become the group's new core but their interests wavered once Paul and Wendy's had. I was almost co-ordinating the group's occasional meetings single-handed which wasn't really a problem with this newfound energy buzz I was enjoying.

My relationship with the shady Gideon had not lost its conversational high and we would still get together to discuss things. After the meetings, Paul and the pregnant Wendy would hurry off home to their necessary commitments while I would look forward to the mesmerising engagement with an old man whom I still knew nothing about. My enthusiasm was certainly not rational but then neither was this period of time. The relationship was purely conversational and it seemed I had been programmed to feed off of this liaison like an addictive energy. Even that evasiveness about who he was, was no longer a problem.

Regularly our topics continued, sometimes for hours: religion, science, magic, secret societies and the secrets of the universe were still covered feverishly. I was learning more about his particular sect and what they did, each meeting must have lured me that bit closer. It was a Masonic group that practiced what sounded to me like woodland solaces or White Magic.

Still no name was given, only vagueness, but still I begged to be invited along.

In hindsight, it is always easy to know the questions you should have asked; but I was hypnotised, programmed just like the sleeper who dreams of walking into work naked and doesn't think to question it. Whether Gideon was an actual alien or one of those nature spirits he spoke of masquerading as an old man was impossible to tell, but how would I have had the awareness to ask? It was made to look like I was the one who instigated coming along to his coven. The odd period of time I was experiencing would only be looked upon as a normal albeit vague patch.

Being a loner, it was difficult to confirm with anybody how strange those few months really were. Years later, I did briefly catch up with someone who I went to college with around that time who proclaimed to have avoided me then. They insisted that I was always in a daze and suspected I was on something like LSD. Any communication from me was always babble, apparently. Embarrassing but interesting feedback.

I vaguely remember having something of great importance arranged with Gideon around that time that was to take place very soon. It was obviously my demanded invitation to his Masonic group but there was something more to the event than just invitation. It was to be an initiation, my initiation. The actual date that this ceremony was to take place I cannot recall but I certainly knew at the time, in fact I had the complete itinerary worked out to a T. I briefly remember meeting with Gideon one last time before this event and remember him being particularly fatherly to me checking that I was entirely happy with what I was about to do. I couldn't have been more certain about anything and felt a glazy-eyed determination to embark.

A certain code and itinerary had been worked out for me, which I would follow like clockwork. All I really remember after my last meeting with Gideon was that buzz, really looking forward to my invitation into his coven which I knew by no conscious instruction meant initiation. No plan that was devised for me was too difficult to take on nor would I question it. I had tunnel vision and doubt that anyone could have stopped me. What was more, I didn't need to be given a date or appointment as I would simply know when the time came. When the inner hypnotist snapped his fingers or gave a recognisable code word, I would take off machine-like.

It came as no notable surprise when the day actually came. It was one evening in January '96, a night appointment, something I might have known given that these episodes always seem to take place after dark. It came without apprehension or any of the concerned awareness that caused resistance. I knew what it was, where to go and what to do, and the only prominent emotion I remember having was excitement. It arrived with the familiar burning sensation in my head, only this time it wasn't there because of a mental boundary. This was different; it felt like more of a signal to spur me on. Maybe it was a warning signal, a type of defence mechanism put there by the Programmers to remind me that I mustn't have second thoughts. That consideration however could not have been further from the truth.

Before I set off, there was something I had to take with me. The burning sensation was not going to let me leave the house without it. I immediately went to the small door of my boiler cupboard, a place where I often hid valuables in the event of a burglary. I reached down inside to feel my way along a dusty shelf and came across what I expected to find there, a small plastic carrier bag scrunched up into a dusty ridge in the wall. Slowly I pulled the bag out letting its weight drop to reveal the contents which seemed to be lead weights. I honestly had no idea what was inside, I was only aware of its importance. I do remember examining the contents which I suppose must have been a pre-programmed routine check rather than curiosity. I don't recall any great surprise when I came across five mysterious metallic objects inside the bag that resembled batteries. Each was cylindrical with copper coloured coating and roughly the same size as batteries normally used for radios or walkmans. I don't remember where these things came from or ever putting them in my boiler cupboard but their whereabouts were etched firmly in my mind. I placed the objects back into the carrier bag and rolled it neatly into my jacket pocket. What I remember about those objects was that they were not particularly interesting to look at or feel but they held a tremendous significance for the meeting I was about to attend.

I left my flat that evening with this sudden gift of tunnel vision free of any usual concerns such as switching off the gas/closing the street door etc. Nothing mattered other than what I was about to do. It was a frosty night with hardly anybody around which I suppose was a blessing considering this hypnotic state I would have been seen in. I just remember walking much further than I normally would particularly as public transport was available. Instead I seemed to be heading to an area devoid of traffic, more towards the remote areas I had visited so many nights beforehand. This time it wasn't the actual park I ventured to but a small road leading off from it, a non-residential road that I instinctively knew was where I had to be. When I arrived, I saw a car parked further down the road that the same instinct hinted was there to collect me. I could never really explain this intuition, but at that time, a brief memory flashed past me about how I used to nickname this feeling the "spider sense," an intuition used by the cartoon Spider Man. It's funny how I had forgotten that. Perhaps the memories of being in this state only resurface when actually returning to that state much like that of a continuing dream.

I approached the parked car, which I couldn't identify because of the darkness, but there were people waiting inside, the driver, an up front passenger and I think two men in the back. I estimated about 4 and surmised they were all male but I cannot be certain. They saw me approach welcoming me in with the back door swinging open. I slid in next to one of the back seat passengers and recall genuine hospitality as I arrived. I do not recall knowing any of these people. Gideon was not amongst them. These people certainly acted like old friends. I remember reciprocating their friendly conversation, but for the life of me, I cannot remember what was said.

I do remember the car pulling away from the kerb and not making any sound, not even an engine igniting. Another thing that struck me about the car was its interior. It might have seemed a passably modern vehicle from the outside but the inside was far removed from the sleek and compact comforts of modern cars. Inside was very basic but roomy with the seats made of old-fashioned leather. As we drove I noticed a dark outline of the old style steering wheel and upholstery possibly wooden with a shiny circular speedometer. It reminded me of an old family Vauxhall from when I was a child with its hard spacious interior and chrome finishes. The absurdity of these scenarios no longer astonishes me when I look back at them because that absurdity seems to be an essential theme. Had I been in a fully conscious state of mind I too would wonder why these things were the way they were. I have found that this theme of absurdity isn't just there as a deliberate smokescreen to confuse but as an actual mishap of compatibility, something I will explain in a later chapter.

It was also hard to detect where we were driving but I would say the car was heading Westerly, more out of the suburbs and into the sticks. I could not make out any familiar roads or buildings but just see occasional streetlights shining in. Another strange aspect was the total absence of other traffic oncoming or otherwise. The roads were quieter tonight than I had ever seen before and this was eerie. If this route existed anywhere in the physical world then it certainly wasn't local. I certainly don't remember or claim to have been this way since.

Despite the unfamiliarity there wasn't an inkling of apprehension in me and the whole journey's conversation had probably been the most familiar I could enjoy with total strangers. Yet still I fail to remember a single spoken word. The estimated 20 minute journey was winding down into a very rural area where the street lighting became less and I could just about make outlines of nearby trees and bushes. We pulled up into a driveway and remember being told we had arrived despite the fact that no sound of slowing wheels or engines could be heard. I remember seeing a particularly dull building in front that I surmised to be our destination.

At a glance the building could have been old brewery or somewhere disused with its old brickwork and lightless windows. The roof was flat and the inky sky above I could just about decipher.

The inside however could not have been further from its mundane exterior. After being led down a short flight of stairs I came to the most elaborate marble floored corridor I had ever seen with huge halls on either side. The building's appearance from outside didn't seem big enough to house this spectacular vastness unless of course we were underground or the house went back a lot further. Even in this unquestioning state I was in awe at the sheer palace of a home around me. People were everywhere talking in groups, like it was a huge palace ball. I would have expected to have seen aristocratic costumes and wigs worn in this scenario but that wasn't the case. The people were dressed exactly as I had been expecting them to on my way over, in Masonic gowns.

Ceremonies seemed to be going on in the halls and I gathered they were being staged for a number of people besides me. I felt that a large process was going on involving batches of people, possibly a routine much like a cattle market. My part seemed to be no more than another subject attending and nobody had even paid much attention to my arrival. Mysterious activity surrounded me.

It wasn't long before I was ushered into one of those halls by someone who offered me a gown to wear exactly like what everyone else wore. I vaguely remember asking my usher if I could wear my jacket under the gown as it contained something very important for the ceremony. She somehow seemed to know what that something was and assured it would be all right. I stood waiting in a queue amongst others as it seemed more like a cattle market now than at first and those queuing were no more aware than cows. Nobody seemed to know why they were there and the interesting thing was the identical look upon their faces. Each of them had an appearance of being in a hypnotic trance mixed with a look of blissful distance. Perhaps I looked that way. Judging by the unsuited confidence I felt and the dreamy look of others, I would say that a great deal of trouble went into keeping us this docile and doubt it was drugs.

What I remember as I stood there was the magnificence of the hall. It wasn't unlike a stately home. The floor was marble like the corridor only this seemed more mosaic similar to the floors found in Roman houses. The ceiling was unnervingly high and decorated with a gorgeous design that I can't quite remember. I recall the walls having flowing red curtains at intervals and even oil paintings that perhaps a connoisseur of art might recognise, but I didn't. Nothing about the event really added up and there I was robbed of the capacity to even question it.

This aspect in itself was fascinating and characteristic. When I think back to how I felt on the occasion, I realise it was pure Oz. The whole scenario had all the Oz Factor's dreamy inconsistencies where if a pink dinosaur had emerged from one of those walls, I wouldn't have criticised it. My head was engulfed with a hazy "not here" feeling, only this was all real. I recall the rough texture of the gown rubbing against the back of my neck, clearly hearing voices speak of all tones and accents and a bizarre smell of incense burning from somewhere. Then of course there was that familiar phenomenon I experienced in all the scenarios, the light. There it was, but where did it come from? No spotlights, bulbs or candles were visible from anywhere yet the light around me was apparent. I have never been hypnotised but suspect this feeling was related to the twilights of a trance.

When I try, I can vividly picture some of the faces I remember seeing that night in the crowd. One of them I will never forget—the one that almost startled me out of my trance. I must have been briefly scanning the list of faces of those in front at queue I was standing. When I came to a familiar one, it almost screamed out at me, not because I knew them personally but because it was a celebrity. From about twenty places in front as the queue wound around to a facing wall it took me a while to register who the person actually was. There as clear as daylight, I saw a reasonably well known British actress standing, waiting her turn like the others and just as dazed. I later wondered what on earth she was doing there and what her connection was but now I doubt there was one. Judging by her entranced look I doubt she actually knew she was there to this day. She seemed so distant of her involvement, the same way I was for most of my life. Perhaps I was the only one who actually recognised her, since no one else gave her second glance while queuing. Why would a famous person attend a gathering like this in such a state particularly when there was enough risk from the press getting wind of it, let alone the general public?

I now realise that this is an on-going programme where large quantities of people are selected (for whatever criteria) and taken outside their awareness to places of a deliberate façade. This time I imagine it was a stately home or at least somewhere of human reference that the experiencer might only look back upon as a strange dream. As clever as these facades may be, their designers sometimes leave inconsistencies such as the source-less light. Only when one tries to recall these scenarios in detail do they spot leaks that appear quite alien. If the controllers of this scenario are as alien as I think they are then perhaps they weren't even aware that this woman was somebody famous. She was perhaps acknowledged as just another of their herd of unquestioning cattle. I have since seen this actress many times on TV and in magazines and fortunately she may not have an inkling of where she really was that night or of her possible involvement in this covert programme. I intend to keep it that way and will not disclose her name. All I will say is that she is an actress, probably not recognisable outside of the United Kingdom. As a person who values privacy, I can only empathise with the vulnerability this would cause.

The evening was peculiar and its time and sequence were always difficult to account for. I remember only outstanding facets, one of them being when my queuing in the line of cloaked people was finally over. I was briskly ushered over to a sectioned off square in the floor where I finally came into contact with my old friend and mentor Gideon. Although I expected him to be there and had seen him recently, it felt emotional. It felt as though I would see him for the very last time and had to bid him farewell. He was dressed like I and everyone else in the hall was and this seemed to emphasise the occasion and its significance. I only recognised him when I looked closer into his hood and it occurred to me what a vital member he must have been of what appeared to be staff.

I remember feeling sad as we hugged like it would be the last time we met. It still baffles me how this elusive stranger had rapidly became an integral part of my life in a such a considerably short time and here I was, heartbroken to see him go. It wasn't as if this scene was even the centre of attention because a buzz of activity went on everywhere, a process involving others queuing the same way as I had and being seen or registered much like the process of an immigration office. I could not detect similar emotion in their quarters that existed in mine.

Much conversation took place between me and the old man but I only remember hearing my voice quaver. I can vaguely remember his responses where he repeatedly reassured me, "You deserve to know. Your time has to come." Whatever he meant didn't convince me, nor could I accept it was his time to depart and I pleaded with him to stay. If this was a dream, it must at least have been premonition as that was the last I would ever see of the man named Gideon.

Time had lapsed again and the next thing I knew I was standing in yet another quarter with three other cloaked figures. I was no longer emotional and didn't feel the same kinship with these beings. They were quite different to many of the other human-like entities in the hall and I suspect they carried out different functions. My impression was that the seemingly human cloaked beings like Gideon who allowed their faces to be seen acted as the kinder ushers and usherettes of the occasion while the shorter shrouded beings might have been the masters. They seemed more efficient but not as sincere as the human-like ones. Their dress was for an occasion that clearly reflected something Masonic and when I think back it spooked me somewhat how they resembled the American Ku Klux Klan. If it wasn't for the alien nature of their actual rituals, I might have even hazarded a guess as to what they may be.

A process was taking place, this time involving the cylinders I had mysteriously harboured still in my inside pocket. I was asked to produce them by one of the beings. He was short like the other two and it struck me how they were nearly identical in size. The now hazy light caused their hoods to cast shadows over their faces making it impossible to see even an outline of a face. I just knew that whatever lurked under that hood was an extremely unappealing sight by human tastes and I have always suspected this to be the reason for their masked faces.

I was asked to produce the battery objects from inside my pocket still wrapped in that plastic bag. I wasn't even given a name for what they were and cannot remember a verbal instruction. His cloak would have made lip reading an impossibility so this only left the conclusion of telepathy, the technique I had engaged in hundreds of times before.

I placed my hand to the bottom of the bag and brought out the five battery-like cylinders as requested. I noticed they were unusually warm as if coming out of a charger. As my fingers rubbed along their copper coating I noticed an odd tingle that wasn't there before when handling them. It seemed that the closer I came to passing them over, the warmer and more electrified they became. The being who had asked me for the objects presented me with this flat board instrument that I seemed to know something about. That board, resembling a coat of arms was a type of ceremonial tool used for collecting the small cylinders. I do not know of the reason for this or why I even had these objects in the first place but understood it to be an essential part of the ritual. One by one I placed the cylinders into the available holes circling the perimeter of this board and felt the objects tingle increase as I did so. Just like a coat of arms, the board was oval shaped with the pronounced edges and also made of some dark wood that was plated with a metallic insignia. Whatever the device was, it seemed electrical. The cylinders slid perfectly into each hole in its formation leaving a kind of static on my fingers. Just slowly placing one in each hole seemed a closely scrutinised and significant task for the ceremony.

Although the ritual was being observed by the three beings, I cannot say it involved anyone else in the hall. Similar events went on elsewhere that were a procedure like mine. This seemingly unique event was probably just an administrative task for the coordinators of the oddity. How often did this happen? Where was it even taking place?

The coat of arms was taken away from me immediately after loading it with the cylinders. There didn't seem to have been any order in which to do this as the holes were identical. I was then asked to turn round and face another part of the room where one of the beings stood in front of me. He/she asked me to go down on one knee as if to receive a knighthood. I can't ever remember misunderstanding an instruction; each one seemed unusually clear. Telepathy was used throughout. Not only did the capacity for questioning seem absent but messages were received as if transmitted directly. Robotically I had gone down on one knee facing the direction I had been asked, awaiting the next instruction. Without rehearsal I went through the perfect motions of a ceremony and the being stood over me as if to offer a simulated knighthood.

Whatever way I had been programmed, I reserved the capacity to observe. Looking past the waist level of the entity's monk-like gown I could see other people queuing along the facing wall just like I had done earlier. Each still possessed that look of vacant trance and I couldn't see that actress anywhere by now. The being was saying something to me, not necessarily instruction but more like a kind of chant which I strangely remember getting the gist of.

The final part of this ceremony involved the being bringing down what seemed to be a square object upon my head. From somewhere he had acquired a metallic shape that resembled a windowpane and this was supposed to be lowered down over me starting from the crown of my head. The action itself wasn't unlike the way security staff at my company occasionally run metal detectors over staff leaving the building in the event of theft only this was different. Here I could actually feel the magnetism of the object. As the shape was lowered over my head I remember feeling the weighty underwater pressure around my temples following a sudden blue crack of light the colour of a camera flash.

That sudden light was hauntingly familiar and I was starting to realise why. Camera flashes have often proved to have an adverse effect on me when having my picture taken. They conjure up memories of odd sensations, flashes from strange stick-like devices—magic wands that leave your eyes burning. If only I could remember what that light signified. I knew it overwhelmed your eyes leaving you fazed and it either made you remember things or forget. Camera flashes and magicians with wands rang so many loud bells, yet I don't remember a thing about this magical square.

I knew it made my head crackle and this (not unpleasant) sensation was accompanied with the flashes. In this case it seemed to provoke memory rather than suppress it and those memories shot at me like rapid déjà vu. Odd things were coming into my thought processes abnormally fast, all due to this thing encompassing my head. Images and emotions came and went faster than I could comprehend. It was like one of those clips seen on TV where a multitude of images are flashed before the viewer leaving them unable to process even one. At rocket speed the images cascaded through my mind, some familiar, some not, a few deeply personal and others notably irrelevant. Had I sat down with a pen and notebook afterwards I could not have written a single thing I had seen. This struck me as interesting gap between the conscious and subconscious, an area which the Programmers have obviously learned to bridge. On a different level, my mind worked as fast as the activity happening to me. Just like the game show contestant who has to remember a whole itinerary of items but can only name one or two afterwards. Hypnotise him and he will remember them all! Could this be the reason that so many alien interactors choose to liaise with these dark parts of the human brain? I seemed to have been processing these images as quickly as I was registering them, yet I would always confess to being the type that likes to digest things in their own time.

The memories were complex but if I was asked to define their whole purpose or meaning I would point to realisation. For about the period of a few minutes, the time I estimated the whole strange event with the square taking place, it seemed to be a session of total and simultaneous realisation. As soon as that blue light cracked around me, I seemed to grasp a huge host of information, some of it familiar and most of it foreign. It was a few minutes where I would say, "So that's what it's all about." I knew the whys and the hows behind most strange things. This was a powerful tool of activation and something I would not only compare with instant knowledge being charged into my brain but a soluble understanding of that knowledge. There is a sad side to this phenomenon because I don't have the means to access that realisation. Some of it still comes back to me at intervals but nothing like those vital minutes of insight.

I say it's sad because I always imagined new knowledge to be permanent, allowing the new awareness forever but that wasn't the case. I have always considered the concept of thought to be intangible but there seem to be beings advanced enough to treat it like magnetic data and actually manipulate it that way. It also comes across as sad how nothing would ever be sacred in a possible future where innermost thoughts could be uploaded and downloaded if that is what was happening. Perhaps it's a blessing that a process like that can only be carried out by highly intelligent and responsible beings, which is the way I view these entities. Otherwise, it would be a frightening violation.

Only recently I had a vague flashback of one of the memories triggered that night and it seemed to be something involving a huge and complex circuit board of some kind. God only knows what this mechanism operated but I remembered understanding it very well. It was another one of those flashbacks occurring while dropping off to sleep. I woke up wondering why nobody had thought of that design before; I even grabbed the pen and pad next to my bed (something I now keep regularly) but it was no good, the fuzzy déjà vu effect wore off before I could collect its magnificence. I was left knowing as much about circuitry as before.

The memory induction ritual with that windowpane device had proven to be the most important part of the ceremony if not of all time during my life of strangeness. It also seemed to be the last oddity I would encounter. I remember the process drawing to a close. The crackling seemed to die down along with the frequency of blue light. The cloaked beings had watched the process although I don't remember them actually commenting or doing anything. When it was over, one of them had reached above me to collect the device and when I think back to this, it was interesting. If one of them had lowered it over my head in the first place why would they have needed to let it go? Had it taken off on its own accord, revolving around my head as I had suspected or was it attached to something?

I recall being very hazy at this stage. New people came over to collect me. These seemed to be the "hosts" consisting of seemingly sincere men and women whom I remember being very praising towards me and offering an assurance that I had done well and it was now all over. That seemed to be a kind of welcoming blur for me after stepping off a highly disorientating fairground ride. I am not sure what really happened afterwards or who put me to bed that night. For me, it was indeed all over and I suppose this largely brings me to the end of my story.

What you will now read are accounts and memories of incidents from my past, the personal history that I thought I knew prior to this ceremony.

Whatever had happened on that night must have been the climax to a very slow period of activation starting from that strange morning where I woke in the park until now.

To my knowledge, no contact or bizarre interaction has taken place since that night of the ceremony, but that doesn't mean that strange memories have stopped seeping through. Maybe I have chosen to write this book at a stage too early in my life because I strongly suspect that the activation is something which continues to this day.

4

Living Programme

Whereas before and only through error had I caught a glimpse of the magic inside Pandora's Box, the lid had now been deliberately blown and its contents saturated me.

Instead of being provided with the answer to everything, it first brought only further confusion. I wasn't transformed from disciple to messiah as one would imagine because my new "gift of enlightenment" didn't appear to have any immediate use. The morning after that strange ceremony (and I cannot even remember that morning) I didn't necessarily rush out to tell the world, in fact I only remember being subdued during this period.

Memories would come to me in unexpected doses similar to the way they had before, only this time, the spoon fed deliverance of those messages seemed to be carefully administered. When I first suspected alien activity in my life it caused me to run before I could walk but now they had left me with an un-manned yet accurately prepared programme that left no room for those unprepared glitches. Clearly my revelation of the "school medical room" seemed to upset the applecart somewhere and someone had decided on a different approach. I imagine that a careful process was planned right from the beginning. First the preparation, second the activation, and third, the rest of my life with its gradual release of memory.

I wanted all that information there and then but for reasons concerning my well-being, not to mention the secrecy of my interactors, that wasn't to be. An acorn had been seeded in me with an oak tree's potential but that alone wouldn't prove the existence of that tree nor its wisdom. I had to wait, stage by stage, and I didn't particularly like it.

The information that was released however was never disappointing and amongst it seemed to be telltale signs about the Programmers and their reality. It is true that they devised a foolproof system this time that wouldn't leak excess information but that wasn't going to control the way I read into it. Among the very first messages secreted into my mind during this process, I gleaned information that wasn't meant to be shared, something about one of their greatest secrets—amnesia.

It occurred to me that these beings didn't come from a reality like we do where time is linear and the sequence is 1 then 2 then 3. Perhaps their past, present and future all exists as one. I have heard this theory discussed a number of times before in UFOlogy and its writing. Quite often in UFOlogy when the subject arises about the home or source of inter-dimensional beings, a "simultaneous time zone" seemed to be a popular theory. I often wonder why alien interaction seems so cryptic and absurd? Imagine for instance how easy it would be for somebody of that "all at once zone" coming to our reality and to manipulate our time line and memories. It's as easy for a playwright to readjust the sequence of events and character's roles to suit a particular outcome. This theory points us right in the direction of explaining many "unexplainable" phenomena, such as déjà vu.

Because we are so used to thinking in terms of linear time and sequence, our memories are fundamental and easy to alter. If these beings were capable of time travel (a theory I sometimes use to explain away the strangeness of my life) they probably wouldn't even need to attempt it for altering our memories. As far as we're concerned, time only exists in a system of 1-2-3 and that gets rearranged as easily as film on a video cassette.

I was only aware that I fell asleep in the park that night in the autumn of '94 followed by a peculiar dream. After that I woke up in the same spot, none of the wiser. The "before and after" sounded plausible enough—but where was the in-between?

This is what I discovered about the aliens and their uses of amnesia. It manifests as some sort of "time theft" for effectively carrying out abduction and is something I am going to refer to as "disorientation." When a person's cognitive skills are disorientated the way mine had been, they could be just about anywhere. It is as simple as returning somebody's awareness back to the point they last remembered and in my case it was collapsing that night onto the grass. The last thing I consciously recalled was feeling excessively tired and only intending to lie down for a few minutes. Whenever my mind tried to think back along that timeline, it always returned to that very moment.

If I thought that little bit harder I would catch a very strange glimpse about memories that never were. Following this comes a familiar burn that tells me I have crossed the line again.

It seemed like a mental default, the way my mind swung back to that moment in the park, discarding all the fuzzy strangeness thereafter as a dream. I knew there was more because it continued to nag me so. Like many other abduction scenarios, it seemed that the aliens had gone to certain lengths to keep me from suspicion whenever I awoke. There is a recurrent theme in abduction cases where the abductors always try to return their subject the way they had found them whether that be in the same place, the same position or even a feeble attempt to redress the abductee had their clothes been removed. There have been many bungled examples of this where abductees wake the next morning with their pyjamas worn back to front or even folded neatly at the bottom of their bed. This proves how their techniques are not as infallible as they seem and I will discuss this "fallibility" later to at least offer hope.

By returning their subjects to the place or scene where they had found them, the aliens can indeed disorientate and banish their victim's suspicion. To make the amnesia effective, I believe they do something more, something to their minds, a "blotting" technique where the secret events are overlapped rather than erased and the very last thing the victim will remember is firmly (telepathically) etched into their minds. It's not impossible to remember the overlapped events but by doing so, the abductee will hit a kind of barrier as I had. I think that the vast majority of abductions are successfully carried out this way and perhaps the ones we read about are the few bungled attempts arousing suspicion. A frightening thought. Particularly when we think about the scale in which this might be happening. Consider how nobody has discovered what déjà vu actually is, yet every one of us has them. Disorientation works, perhaps on a disturbing scale.

It wasn't until after the "activation" encounter at the secret ceremony that I became aware of this practice. I started to recognise a certain trait about its effects. You only recall things when you truly want to do so. I possessed knowledge, the type of knowledge that certain people in high places would have me killed for, yet I went about my business as though nothing had happened. That newly charged knowledge was just random data lying dormant and it would only take a certain trigger to stimulate it. It must have been about a fortnight after the secret ceremony that the first of those trigger memories came to me.

It was one particular evening where I strolled through a shopping mall taking advantage of the Thursday night trading. I remember just casually browsing through household goods for my flat when I came across a particular display in one of the shop windows, a display of lava lamps. Like most children of the 70's, I grew up with those mesmerising lava lamps which had all of a sudden become very chic again. But something seemed to have grabbed me that wasn't just nostalgia. I looked at the contents of one of the lamps on display showing the usual amber bubbles rising and bobbing and I was gripped by their colour and mutating effect. That night in the park last autumn I was actually being pursued by something like that! Not so much the lava lamp but one of its bubbles, in fact it changed shape and colour the same way that those things do. How could I have forgotten that? My memory of the sky coming alive that night and resembling a lava lamp was not a dream.

I didn't go straight home that evening. I wandered around absorbed in my fascinating new memory. This is how I now remembered that incident in the park: I seemed to have been going there on a regular basis but that evening I was going to meet someone. I felt pursued by flickering balls of light that would disappear whenever I looked at them. I remember seeing the sky become a type of liquid revolving around a certain nucleus shaped like a crescent. Whenever that crescent moved, everything seemed to follow. Its surroundings were affected and so was I. It changed shape and colour exactly like those bubbles of oil in the window display, only it seemed to have a central purpose, which I suspect was me. I remembered a mist around the craft and even though its amber light was dimly lit, it hurt my eyes. The structure of that shape went from a formless bubble to an oval although it seemed to prefer its crescent shape and reverted back to that often. It slowly cascaded its colours from its primary dim yellow to a brilliant red followed by a rich green. After green, it faded into white making everything around it that colour and then the formation would begin again.

My familiar surroundings of Richmond Park were becoming less convincing. Whatever that craft did in the sky seemed to affect all around it. I remembered how an outline of trees in the distance had almost become absorbed into the night sky and although night had fallen, the activity above still caused a daylight effect. The craft's rotation of colours had now become less frequent and everything seemed to linger more in the white. This colour was causing an odd sensation around me, and not just a visual one. The whiteness seemed to be an energy absorbing everything. There was something hauntingly familiar about that white light.

Not only did the whiteness have a dense consistency to it that obscured my vision of everything, even the grass below, but it also absorbed sound and movement. I had that dreamlike sensation of moving through liquid, and although white light blanked out everything visible, I could strangely see myself, my own hands in front of me. Sounds become drowned out and distant where my own footsteps on the leaves below sounded as they might with fingers in my ears. I couldn't even describe this light as a fog because even our traditional "pea soup fog" was never this consistent. The best analogy I can give is something like being inside a lit argon bulb and still being able to see. This light was an energy in itself robbing the five senses and blanking out all except the craft and myself. The object above was the nucleus of everything and the only spot where the white consistency broke. I had the impression that the craft and I were the last two occupiers of reality.

This white realm was a strange and familiar place that always seemed to happen as a prelude to something even stranger. Years later, during my research, I ploughed through a number of books on the paranormal and read about many familiar sensations but none identical to this white limbo that I had often plunged into during encounters. Maybe it wasn't anything external but an induced state of my mind. Perhaps everybody's is different.

It was during the whiteness that I became incredibly tired and wanted to lie down. The craft still pulsated above with a brilliant white with a hypnotic effect on me. Normally when I think back to this part of the story, the disorientation creeps in and catapults me forward to the time I wake up but that wasn't going to happen. Something took place while in the docile state, the one I called a dream.

It began as one of those "swimming" dreams where one can do the breaststroke in mid air. I swam or was drawn upwards towards what looked like an opening in the craft's underside. To swim away from this opening would have been like resisting a strong current towards a plughole but I don't remember even trying. In fact the experience felt more tranquil than threatening. I only remembered feeling vaguely concerned that I was too drowsy for the task ahead, instinctively knowing there was a task ahead. Out of nowhere came a voice of reassurance the moment the doubtful thought entered my mind, something to the effect of "Stay calm, you won't be asked to do anything."

I remembered thinking either to myself or if in response to the source-less voice how relieving that was to hear. I could hardly keep my eyes open.

Feeling myself pass through what seemed to be a portal in the object (only identifiable by a different tone of light) felt briefly familiar, like slowly drawing a tissue from a box of handkerchiefs. There have been a number of times where my entire self felt as light and versatile as tissue, which I will explain later when I try to analyse the astral side. Without the unexplained pull coming from this portal, I honestly felt light enough to be blown away by a breeze.

The next thing I knew, I was confronted with a type of welcoming committee all dressed in the familiar robes and pointed hoods. I couldn't see where I actually was as the room I arrived in appeared to be in a mist like a mild sauna allowing me to hardly see anything other than this small gathering of people. Each of them appeared to be doing something to me, something to my clothes, which I was astonished to find, weren't my own. As I looked down I only saw that brown robe, worn many times before on these occasions. I could only surmise that time had passed since being drawn up through that hole and waking here, it seemed like they had just finished dressing me.

I remember how my first thoughts were of death, particularly with the religious theme of those outfits and the mist. Perhaps I had passed over to the other side and was being greeted by holy men or angels even. It wasn't the first time that I noticed the shocking similarities between their appearance and the Grim Reaper who is said to visit those about to die. It often makes me wonder where and why that archetype came about.

Communication had already begun. I knew I was contributing. I must have wondered about this object I had floated into because I asked unusually direct questions:

"Is this some sort of spaceship? Are you those magician people I used to play with?"

With telepathy the reply is instantaneous: "Your knowledge is expanding too much and it will harm you. Try to trust us and we will make you better, happier."

I cannot be sure if those were the exact words but that is how I interpreted it. Although it seemed an irrelevant answer with hints of Double-Dutch, it coveys more to me now than I ever believed it would. I also believe that my questions were being answered in their abstract technique of demonstration. I was led into another room that appeared to be a studio of some kind, far more hi-tech than the steam (arrival) room. They were definitely trying to bring something home to me regarding that comment about expanding knowledge. That seemed to be the whole reason I was there, my earlier defiance about learning too much about them at a premature stage. "It will harm you." I had been subliminally warned on several occasions not to go down that inquisitive path but my suspicion would have none of it. This was probably the final warning in the form of a "mind alteration."

The alien way of communication uses gestures, documented images and scenarios. I stood in this studio type room with about five of the cloaked beings standing around me, waiting for something. At this point I noticed that the room seemed bigger than I first imagined but that was due to something else happening. There was a whole new phenomenon taking place where I could experience two different scenarios, one inside with the beings and another existing in an outside location far removed from where I actually was. When I looked around me I was in a strikingly convincing scene of a garden somewhere with other people around me. Yet if I looked beyond this, I could see the perimeter of the room and the cloaked beings watching me. They seemed to have induced some state of dual vision where I could quite convincingly be in two places and whichever one I chose to focus on turned out to be the realistic one.

For some reason they wanted me to interact with or at least experience the one they had imposed as this was where a message lay waiting. It seemed more appeasing than the reality of their featureless room as this scene appeared to be one of greenery and sunlight. When I chose to focus on the images, the room's background and the beings within it deteriorated miraculously. I was back in that garden with those other people watching a strange commotion going on. It showed a group of doctors or medical nurses trying to restrain a hysterical patient displaying a fierce resistance to something. The man (no one I seemed to know) in his fifties seemed genuinely fearful and was constantly babbling out loud something hard to decipher, a foreign language perhaps. It was difficult to say what vantage point I was standing at because I was able to view the scene at all angles. Everything was three-dimensional to look at except for myself, I seemed to be no more than a viewpoint in this scene and saw no evidence of what I actually was. I studied the scene displayed to me suspecting that my abductors were testing me. At first the odd scene of doctors restraining a patient didn't have any relevance until something horrible dawned upon me; the patient in question could have in some representative way been me.

It was hard to see myself in this man but I was overcome how intriguing and disturbing it was that someone else (aliens) saw me this way. I even remember an old saying coming to mind, "Grant us the gift to see ourselves the way others see us." How many people can honestly say they've had the faculty to see themselves from another perspective, the way we see others? It also disturbed me what actually went on in the scene because this was never a replay of anything happening in my life. The man was clearly freaked out and one of the nurses prepared a syringe of tranquilliser for him while the others maintained a desperate restraint. Also disturbing was the way he ranted about something that I couldn't understand a word of. The ranting was not even a language I could understand or identify.

He was eventually subdued with one arm held outwards for the nurse to inject. The brief and explosive scene died down with what appeared to be dwindling rants still trying to say something. I remembered the feeling of sadness as my mind tried to register some sort of meaning behind it all.

The message reiterated by the beings: "Expanding knowledge can do harm." The penny had dropped through one of their mind games.

That scene never had nor ever will take place. It was a psycho-dramatic possibility of what to expect if I learned too much too soon from this "spill over" of information. That was why I had been abducted that night. The strange language spoken by the patient is something I'll never know.

Before the tranquilliser showed any effect on the sad image of the dwindling man, I was whisked away on to yet another scene. Like the previous, I didn't appear to have any vantage point and remained just an anonymity with the ability to view all angles.

This time it was a scene of busy street (no particular street that I knew) that showed people going about their daily business. I remembered seeing traffic, pedestrians and the usual sight of people engaged in everyday activity, but there was something odd. Things were taking place outside of the activity shown and the people were not even aware of it. As I looked upon what seemed to be a family crossing the road, there were ghostly people walking in midair right above them. Scores of nearly transparent people were everywhere in the scene together with ghostly inanimate objects such as vehicles passing right through the physical ones. I seemed to be witnessing another dual reality where the occupants of each were totally oblivious to one another. The ghostly reality reminded me of those images sometimes seen on faulty TV sets and photographs. One existence seemed to be intertwined with the other and only I, the onlooker, seemed to be aware. An impression immediately came to mind, accompanied with this scene, something about "belief and evidence." The message: "It is reality. How could I ever define it and why should I even try to prove it exists?" At this point I remember having the wind drawn completely from my sails.

If this is the way it was in everyday life, then we must be tiny cogs in the works of a frighteningly large and complex network. If anybody actually knows of this "other" reality then they would probably be in peak of authority and my life didn't even touch upon that status. Even suggesting this to anyone would leave me without a leg to stand on because none of it truly exists in our realm, the physical. What I looked upon was a kind of inter-dimensional world, a hypothetical one almost. And the message gained through their usual psycho-dramatics: "You have been plunged into something way above your head, try to forget it, you're just not ready." Through the disappointment came a personal acceptance and it wasn't until I swallowed that acceptance that we shifted yet again.

I find this "scene shifting" miraculous. All of a sudden as if no time had passed, I was in another room with another cloaked entity, wearing my ordinary clothes this time. Time had passed because I already seemed to be in conversation with the being. This time I got the impression that messages of condolence or morale were being offered:

"Now you see why we had to bring you here. Try not to worry about us or our world. Live your life as we will always be here. Abandon your pursuit of these things and forget the disappointment. Live on, etc."

My recall of these messages made no sense to begin with but after repeating them to me, they seem to point to a bigger picture. The two "virtual reality" scenes that had been shown were a subtle way of converting my interests. My persistent intrigue beforehand was causing problems for them and their security. Something had to be done with me, mentally. I suspect they would have had the means to simply erase the knowledge from my mind if they wanted but perhaps that was too crude. They had to make me "want" to come around to their way of thinking and the two scenes shown were an effective way of doing that. The first scene involving the doctors being a kind of "shock documentary" of what might happen whilst the second one would remind me of how intangible and remote their reality actually was. Both were tools for influencing discouragement and both had worked. It would certainly explain the out-of-character cynicism I acquired around that time and my sudden doubts of the paranormal.

The one faculty they had left me with was my vibrant intrigue, the driving force behind the formation of CE5. I suspect that had been left deliberately so that my mind would always be kept open, perhaps for future contact?

I will never really know if that cloaked being was actually Gideon, my now departed friend and mentor. I did after all discuss certain things in depth during that abduction the way I did with Gideon where messages were transmitted and immediately understood without so much as a pardon. Some of those messages I have managed to convert into chosen words or phrases of our language. The gist of the messages are what I have highlighted above. This is as accurate as I can be given the incomprehensibility of all things telepathic.

"He" seemed to be my last person to liaison with on that bizarre trip as it looked as though it was my time to depart. It was at this point that

I remembered where those mysterious battery objects I possessed came from. I remembered him giving me something like a handful of metal chips almost as a farewell. He convinced me that the objects held a particularly special purpose, something to do with "collection" and that I needed to keep them for a while. His instructions were well followed.

On reflection I have a fair idea of what he meant by "collection." An impression came to me of a method I could compare to psychometry, the technique used to study a person's past present and sometimes future using objects they possess such as jewellery. The objects were not necessarily attached to me like jewellery instead only left in my house but that apparently was enough to collect whatever "vibes" I may have transmitted.

I clearly remember collecting them from the cupboard where my gas appliance was but don't remember actually putting them there. In fact, the moment that being presented them to me was all I really remembered of the objects.

In an instant, that scene changed to another without a transition. This new scene hurt my head slightly when I try to recall it because of "disorientation." I remember seeing light similar to the light I first witnessed where everything went white and all I could see was the luminous amber blob with the sky resembling liquid. The same tiredness consumed me and I couldn't resist passing out. Before I could comprehend anything, I remembered feeling dry grass beneath me while turning over to try to see the odd light again. Nothing. Stupid dream were the only words I remember, whether they were my uttering or someone else's. Stupid dream seemed quite reasonable as I recall the weariness pulling me back down into a deep sleep.

Upon waking, the only fragments of memory I had were of a dream and the only image coming to mind seemed to be that amber blob. Just thinking about that at the time with its accompanying white light seemed to hurt my eyes and querying it only activated that mental boundary, making my head hurt even more.

That was my memory—alien disorientation, psycho-dramatic scenes and mental programming, all fantastic feats of engineering possible from another realm. Where did any of this leave me? That night, since seeing the oil lamps, I remained lost in thought and wandered around until late.

Never has such an astounding event buried in my mind come back with such impact and clarity. This was the beginning of a whole new era in my life where I had been granted unconditional scope to explore the past and my mind without boundaries. The night in the park was the first of a bizarre flood of memories that would leak to the surface at the most unexpected times.

That night I seemed to have slept far better than normal. The revelation must have been taxing. I used the following few days to collect myself and take it easy. There wasn't a single doubt in my mind now that a huge part of my past was spent partaking in alien activities.

It all seemed to fit perfectly well when I thought back to the strangeness of everything. All along, the wool had been pulled over my eyes until a time when I suddenly recalled a strange childhood memory of a school medical room incident. That memory hinted some involvement with the paranormal, my subject of fascination and that triggered a relentless intrigue to uncover things. It appeared to be a slip up made by someone and they obviously didn't appreciate my investigation. More information was coming through and soon the horse would have bolted too much to allow the stable door to close. A number of psychological attempts were made to divert my mind from this information "expanding knowledge harming you" and I must have been stubborn because the last resort seemed to have been finally called for, the night in the park- alien abduction.

From what I remember whilst aboard that suspended vehicle, everything was meticulously planned as a last measure to reprogram my mind. It obviously worked. Overnight I seemed to have been transformed with a whole new mental outlook.

A new chapter began where my interests and horizons were pleasantly broadened. A man named Gideon suddenly arrived in my life as mysteriously as he exited it and I can only assume he had been "sent" either as someone to overlook or a guardian angel perhaps. In fact, he was the most outstanding piece to my entire puzzle and stood out as a part that didn't fit. He was not an ethereal being or an alien but his presence and regular partaking in my life caused inconsistencies that never added up. Whenever Gideon came into my world he seemed to bring with him the Oz Factor along with all its strange physical laws and indescribable time sequences. My meetings with him didn't make sense, time passed quicker than it ever should and my basic sense of analytical critique shut down whenever I saw him. It could have been a time where I was unwittingly hypnotised or even operating in a conscious dream.

It wasn't until months later following a particular night in January '96 where I was collected by a suspicious car and driven to a Masonic ceremony that a part of that strangeness began to clear. That ceremony was the last incident where I ever saw the mysterious Gideon and my involvement there seemed to be a type of farewell ceremony. Those cylindrical objects I possessed were handed back to the beings as if a token of myself and in return I was granted the gift of memory.

Looking back, it wasn't unlike the religious Bar Mitzvah ceremony where a 13-year old boy attends a special initiation to pass him over to religious manhood. There were certain traits to that ceremony that smacked of our earthly ones, both religious and pagan. It was as if I had proved my own maturity that night and was initialised into a higher level of understanding. After going though such a suspicious and turbulent period I had perhaps now acquired enough wisdom not to yell out to the whole world that I was in touch with the other side. Perhaps now I could contain the knowledge of the beings and their world without going to pieces like I might have done years beforehand.

I had been stringently monitored all the way and every time I slipped off of the rails, I was put back with careful precision. By some omnipotent method, there are overlords who can engineer this. I believe it is carried out from their own ethereal zone where all things are possible, past present and future.

With this new awareness I could gradually unfold the past and make of it what I had to. I still think the most astounding memories were during the abduction where for the first time I had actually seen the physical and technical sides of this phenomenon. That thing I had seen in the sky seemed like a machine both technical and biological. Its structure was like nothing we have in our world as it seemed to become solid or mutating whenever it needed. I even remember seeing a portal in its underside into which I was weightlessly drawn.

However the thing that really blew my mind were those holographic displays shown to me aboard, the images conjured from nowhere. If

I didn't know better I would insist that was the future of virtual reality maybe hundreds of years ahead of our own version. Not even our best technology with the cyber-helmets can totally fool anyone onto believing images are completely three-dimensional and even allow us a view of all angles similar to the way interactive TV does. Their version of VR seems to have moved onto something more convincing than "actual" reality.

The messages intended from those psycho-dramatic scenes may have been cryptic, but they made perfect sense. Even thought the alien beings appear to beat about the bush when delivering a message, this technique gets it across in the most impressionable way. "Psychodrama" as I am calling it might also be the future of communication as it is of virtual reality. For years we have used visual media to demonstrate and bring messages across this way and perhaps what I have witnessed shows an alien reflection of this. What I have seen seems to be a way of life much like telepathy and other bizarre communicative tactics.

Rather than just telling me that I was getting into something too deep and to steer clear only to have me balk and defy, they showed me shock documentaries that would impress upon emotions as well as thoughts. By inducing a scene of a sickly man ranting in a strange language and another of an inaccessible realm, they had impressed upon me a deep message. It was like brainwashing but far more effective—your core self transformed into their way of thinking. "The ranting patient is what happens to those with too much knowledge—the ghostly scene within the earthly one is an example of where our world actually is." That was at least how I interpreted it. "Try to trust us and we will make you better, happier." Steer clear and find other interests and you won't end up this way.

These messages were better subliminal and that explains why I was made to forget the incident aboard the craft. As soon as I was returned to "terra firma", a new mental outlook began in which I would treat these odd paranormal episodes with a pinch of salt. Life seemed to have picked up a great deal after that where I chose to study science rather than just dream about it. My interest in the paranormal remained, although I became quite blasé about any hints of personal involvement. A new no-nonsense and scientific outlook led me to form CE5 and then the saga with Gideon began.

I was collected at an arranged location in an absurd car and driven to a gathering for an even more absurd ceremony. This was the final opening of a secret box where everything suspicious happening in my past was cryptically explained. The visitors of my life were to finally depart and the future seemed to have been left for whatever I wanted to make of it.

The future part is what concerned me the most, because I really wondered what it meant for me now. I felt that these overlords had finally abandoned whatever project it was that had centred upon my life for so long. Their departure had seemed so final and it was like I was now expected to possess their wisdom and knowledge like the bird ready to fly the nest. They were somehow telling me that I had "passed over" and about to take my first steps.

I began to get the gist of what was happening, and why it was happening yet there were still enormous gaps between my knowledge and truly understanding. Nothing is ever explained directly and perhaps that is due to our ability to comprehend, similar to the way we use methods to help animals understand our processes.

I can only imagine what level these beings must operate at to have to communicate in such an obscure and abstract way. I have received messages in the English language through telepathy on so many occasions but I have only ever properly learned of my programme from them by gesture and demonstration.

My impression as the animal was that it was over. For whatever reason, I had been targeted for research right from the beginning with a programme devised for me. In that time, I had been studied, evaluated and finally released back into the wild to make of it whatever I will.

Memory wasn't the only gift they had left me with on their departure. Something had been left in my mind; something intelligently controlled and automated to carefully administer my memories. I couldn't just reach in and extract anything I wanted because the memory facility was now a slow-acting capsule, gradually releasing data when appropriate. My mind still seemed to have its parameters and areas that I couldn't explore even though the Programmers and their intrusion had long left me. I instinctively knew that there was more information buried deep and that it would surface in its own good time. What could this programme have been if it wasn't a living entity? Not living as in conscious or aware but something robotic and time activated that seemed to have its own presence rather like an inanimate counterpart such as a digital clock.

The living programme even had its own defence mechanism much like the mental taboos I spoke of earlier but probably not as strict. I now had the freedom to wonder without the sensation of a "head burn" every time I crossed or queried a set boundary. Now, when my mind chose to wander over those boundaries, nothing really happened. I simply could not remember what I wasn't allowed to and that was its defence. It had all been cleverly engineered so I still had limits yet also a newly given leeway. I doubt that even the most sophisticated hypnotist would have been able to break into this deep and dormant mechanism.

These beings were gone but had left their mark unreachably deep. I surmised that the mechanism wouldn't be there forever. Like most of the alien contrives, given time they always deteriorate without trace. My body and mind had been a vehicle for them to help them operate in our reality.

I had often read of alien encounters where the subject had reported strange and unaccounted marks on their bodies such as incisions or foreign objects under the skin. I have never (consciously) recalled anything as physical or crude as this. Maybe that is due to what I surmised in an earlier chapter about subjects being prescribed different programmes "courses for horses" or maybe even contact with different races of beings. The ones that I had been involved with I suspect were more "mind orientated" and psychologically interactive than physical. I don't ever remember physical examinations being carried out and never come across any strange or unaccounted marks. I always insisted that they only used me as a tool and abandoned me when I became of no further use. I have sensed great compassion and by that compassion I would be able to recognise my particular visitors anywhere. Whether or not I will remains to be seen.

Similar to the reported "Greys" and "Nordics" and various others that seem to display certain patterns in people's lives that typify them, my Programmers had shown an identifiable pattern. Part of that pattern is their psychological presence. I sensed a paternal kindness and wisdom commonly found in a religious elder such as a priest but on the other hand there is that distance making their wisdom seem incomprehensible and out of reach for the likes of a human. Because of that, they will always seem light years away, even in their immediate presence.

Despite that I still miss them. Regardless of their departure without truly explaining who they ever were and all the jumbled and cryptic information they had left me with, I still desired that feeling of enlightenment when being in their company. Perhaps the one I missed most was the elusive contact they seemed to have appointed to me, Gideon. If there was anyone seemingly from this planet who emitted the same paternal, magical presence of the Programmers, he seemed to have had the art. I am convinced he was never human because of the magnitude of his intelligence and the manipulative command that intelligence had over my trust. Remember how he came into my life a total stranger.

Early in '96 when it actually dawned on me that I may never see Gideon again, I desperately searched for his possible whereabouts and origin. I clarified with others such as Paul and Wendy who had actually met the man and how they would describe him. I wanted to confirm he wasn't just a figment of my imagination like countless others I believed to be from my past. Their descriptions and summing up fitted with mine but they could never have truly known him the way I did. Nothing could account for his elusiveness either, the way he first mysteriously came into my life.

I retraced our footsteps from the beginning, that first meeting of the UFO study group held at the community hall to the time of the unexplained ceremony. Nobody seemed to know anything, not the study group or anyone in the area. This didn't surprise me. I knew how this man's tracks would have been covered professionally, almost magically. If Scotland Yard had been on this case they wouldn't have come any nearer. The case was closed and I drew my own conclusions. The man called Gideon was some kind of agent or co-ordinator from the existence I call the Otherness. His techniques pointed to the suspicion that he had interacted with my life all along which is why I thought his face screamed of familiarity the day I met him.

During that period, months after the night ceremony, I seemed to be in a reflective mood with much time on my hands. I used this time to investigate more than just my kinship with Gideon. My whole life had been strange but the strangeness had definitely come to a climax during those last few years. Where exactly was that ceremony held and what about the UFO encounter?

I searched the vastness of Richmond Park and although I came across parts that were vaguely familiar, none were exact. I even tried visiting the park at twilight hours just to get the same feel and help jog memories of the night in autumn '94. The exact location of the event still evaded me. It was easy to remember where I actually walked that night even in my induced daze but the place where it should have led me to just wasn't the one.

With so much time on my hands, I later decided to investigate some other areas of phenomenon only to come to similar results. I was intrigued by that night of the ceremony where I was driven to a strange location in a very questionable vehicle. Finding the spot where I was collected by the car was easy as it was a place I knew well but the route we had taken was a mystery. Each night I would travel top deck on any of the local bus routes to try to identify where I was actually driven that night but nothing looked familiar. I was so eager to find that building where the ceremony took place; the one that resembled a stately home inside but nothing like that existed for miles. I even checked with the local town hall and the nearest one would never have justified my short car journey that night.

These searches reminded me of those black comedies about paranoia where a person tries to go places where an event was supposed to have happened but finds it miraculously removed. I can only put this down to the level of strangeness that one can expect to find when confronted with the odd climates of another existence. It isn't even something I could share with anyone due to its total defiance of logic and physical law. Disorientation of time and location seem to be common traits of this interaction and I cannot really expect anybody to believe me.

I had reached a time in my life of acceptance where the conclusion to something could be satisfactorily met with a question mark. No longer would I rack my brains to try to rationalise a procession of events that were so utterly irrational. I was already convinced of a metaphysical existence where time and distance were immaterial and I wasn't going to look into its mechanisms or even try to explain its mystery. What mattered at this point was that I was far from insane yet these occurrences were very real and not just the product of dreaming. The more I read about these episodes whether they are ghostly or seemingly sci-fi, there seemed to be this common theme of otherworldly conditions where time and physics are quite different. Although I hadn't read of anything identical to my own experiences, so many people involved in these things have reported their own particular version of the "otherness" where life and reality were something else. The way one perceives this is probably quite subjective.

The way in which the paranormal actually affects you can also be personal and characteristic. I seemed to have been experiencing the aftermath of a lifelong paranormal relationship and remember feeling incredibly lonely some time after my visitor's departure. So many times I would find gaps in my life where I believe a mutual activity once took place and remember great confusion about these gaps without even suspecting the presence of others.

In 1996, I first felt specially prepared for the information that was slowly uploading from the depths of my mind. I didn't necessarily go to pieces with the information like I suspected I might; this possibility was also taken care of. Alongside the feelings of abandonment came that acceptance and that was a blessing. My now departed friends had left me with a marvellous and automated device to protect as well as educate.

The living programme seemed to work in accordance with my intellectual and emotional capacity. It was as though the system knew which buttons to press and which ones to steer clear of and in a way, I suspect it was cleverer than the Programmers themselves. I think that when someone is selected the way I had been, the interaction is a long pattern of trial and error. So many slip-ups occur along the way which the visitors themselves have to immediately patch up.

This early period of interaction can last for years and I believe it's like a period of teething troubles for the visitors to get to know their subject. My particular visitors must have needed most of my life to date because they had only just departed.

I have often read of cases where the visitors are reported to have suddenly departed this way without warning, finally leaving their subject to live in peace. Quite often, there are "souvenirs" left over similar to my programme such as those crude tracking devices commonly found in the subject's nasal cavity. I am not entirely sure what the significance of these "leftovers" actually is but I feel that my mental contraption was something quite different. It seemed to be astral as opposed to technical and worked upon the concept of the "mind" rather than the brain. I doubt that even the most advanced of CAT scans that analyse the brain would be able to detect the presence of this device.

Instead of tracking devices, perhaps it is the latest technique of alien implanting following the many foiled examples of the ones that humans have extracted and found to self destruct.

I imagine that my own "auric" version of an implant will also self destruct given time. That will be when my visitors will have truly gone from my life and taken their mark with them. Until then I can only consider myself a marked man with total freedom to roam but able to be detected if necessary. I still regard this freedom a blessing and accept that I can at least theorise about things from now on.

Burning questions remain unanswered, but perhaps that is case with the paranormal and UFOlogy worldwide.

I used this time to try to get my life back in order, but the impact left upon my mind by the visitors seemed to have robbed me of cognitive skills. Whenever the beings made a major presence in my life it seemed to affect my mental state either by boosting or crippling it.

As I was growing up, their subliminal presence always cluttered my mind with unexplained activity that would hinder my concentration and later lead to underachievement. Much later in life my mind gets altered further where I developed a thirst for learning and a new capacity to absorb information. I chose science and discovered abilities I never knew I had. Those distractive obsessions for obscure subjects such as stage magic and the occult managed to take a back seat, which was extremely useful.

I had become a changed person with new connections and resources, someone with a mind open to all possibilities. That was until the recent development took place with the ceremony and the departure of my "friends." Since this happened, my mind seemed to have reverted back to the old limited state in which it had been prior to my awareness. I only discovered this when I tried to pick up the pieces and continue with my life once the dust had settled from my ceremonial affair.

My first thoughts were to extend my studies, particularly as I had done so well with my science degree. I went on a brief refresher course with an intention to further where I had left off, perhaps on to the next level. When I embarked on this study I was completely shocked. That cast iron willingness I developed for learning seemed to have mysteriously withered and I couldn't understand why. My ability to grasp facts and figures also seemed absent and I was left wondering how I ever managed to even get through the absolute basics of the science degree. It really felt as though I was now sitting the studies for another person, the bright student who regularly attended this college the previous year.

Needless to say, I didn't continue with this extended study. It was quite shocking to realise how my mind had reverted back to a time when I really didn't care for anything academic. Just as before, my mind seemed both unsettled and unwilling to apply itself to study, my concentration span resembled an insect's and the new ability to grasp things (a granted gift I believe) seemed to have diminished.

It wasn't for lack of trying or the effects of the recent events that caused this decline as I genuinely felt different. I find it amazing how alien interaction can make or break a person's mind this way but then maybe it was deliberate engineering.

This was another unique and notable point in my saga of interaction. I hadn't read anything exactly like this before. There are a number of cases where people have reported new or creative breakthroughs following exposure to alien intervention or the paranormal where they have taken to art or spirituality. There are also cases where abductees have developed social and ecological consciences and expressed great concerns for the environment, but not once have I come across a case where the gifts are actually taken back.

I felt bare and out on a limb. Somebody had used me all along and then departed leaving me as a shell of who I was before. It even felt like I had been put on a special medication to keep me a certain way. Although I wouldn't have described my state of mind around this time as unpleasant, it was definitely being controlled and even repressed. So often I would find myself in this deeply reflective mood where I could sit and ponder over my cryptic past with the visitors but there also came a terrible lethargy with this state where I would let life pass by.

My zest for science and its study seemed to have long gone and I developed a compulsion for complacency. At the same time there was still the familiar abundance of activity that brought in floods of strange memories. It felt as though I had been turned into a slow-acting machine that could do nothing other than get charged with electrical information and when I look back to this state, I realise there was a reason. Without it I may have cracked into a thousand pieces.

It was undoubtedly some kind of spell I had been put under, one which lasted for a few years. When I think about magical folklore of witches and their bizarre spells cast for either good or bad, it brings home what a spell actually is. Rather than being something that influences a person's luck it moulds their minds, moods and perhaps auras. Unexplained mood swings are not uncommon in people but it is a frightening thought how these states are said to be creatable by humans within secret bodies using crude ELF waves as some conspiracy theorists suggest.

In this state, frequent memories would strike at unexpected moments while something inside safely kept my mind at bay. With these memories and sometimes through a change in emotion, objects around me would occasionally move. There were still times where I would walk past desks and papers would fly towards me, sticking to my back. Spoons and crockery would sometimes shudder as I approached the table and there were occasions where TV and radio were affected by my presence.

This might have been emotionally devastating had I not been in this collective lull of complacency and pondering. I must have meant something to these beings given that they had preserved my sanity this way. I often wonder if that meant they would return at some point in the future to hijack my mind once more using it as an earthly base of operation.

The following few years gave no sign of this whatsoever although it did prove to be an enlightening period in terms of revelation.

5

The Truth in Yesterday

Children and often adults have a tendency to reserve things that they cannot understand. When the human mind fails to comprehend something, it has a habit of stowing it away in a question-marked box for a very long time. It would explain why incidents of child abuse happening at ages where the mind is unable to fully register what's happened often surfaces much later in adulthood.

Personally, I cannot equate what has happened to me as remotely similar to "abuse" but it strikes me how minds have this mechanism to register and accept things that don't necessarily add up. Although I regard my childhood to have been a happy one and unusually sheltered both with and without the experiences, there was nothing within my culture that would have prepared me for the confusion of alien interaction. I use the term "alien" because there is no established term for the astral entities I encountered that so few know about.

Apart from the obvious ridicule, people tend to keep these experiences to themselves mainly because their education or culture has no place for them. "Register and accept with the benefit of the doubt', that was what I had been doing for at least four complacent years following my bombshell revelation in '96. I knew that so much went on behind the scenes of my life that wasn't strictly the product of dreams or ghosts and all along, subliminal string-pullers kept me docile, insisting that I doubted everything. I knew that so much was wrong and out of place yet I remained doubtful, refusing to make an issue of a single thing. That was until the year of 1999 when the "spell" was beginning to wear off.

When that happened, I tried to make head and tale of all the disorientating events of my life by chronicling them and could not believe the list I had made. This is my first proper attempt at writing and even now as I look back upon the ludicrous stories I am telling, all things I insist have happened to me, the disbelief and embarrassment never ceases. The absurdity behind the alien agenda (something I will try to explain) puts the experiencer in a particularly feeble position, leaving them telling a tale that sounds lacking in proper reference to anything. So many times I have been tempted to describe the hooded beings of my childhood as benevolent Martians who have come here to save the world, just to give my story a bit of credibility but nothing is ever that simple. Things have happened that are cryptic and point to the existence of an ethereality, involving the mystery of time and the afterlife.

My slow release of memory, a programme I believe to have been installed, only adds to that peculiarity. When memories of missing time or disorientated events resurface, it completely rewrites the way you acknowledge yesterday. I found that things came to me in that very disconcerting déjà vu sensation making me want to turn around and say, "Oh, that's how it happened." Often things were not as I remembered them and it leaves me puzzled as to how I could have ever forgotten them that way.

There was a particular scene from a recent sci-fi movie that touched upon my interpretation of altered memories. In the film "Frequency", a film about time travel, a man had his past altered so that new memories suddenly came to him leaving the old ones to appear as events that never were. (Déjà vu?)

> "*My father didn't die in a fire-fighting incident back in 1969, he died more recently of a heart attack.*"

Much to the confused horror of his colleagues who were only too aware of the facts he blurted out, he was left wondering why he said it. That is how new memories come to people who have experienced missing or overlapped time. That isn't to say that time travel is actually used, it's more to do with how the Programmers manipulate the mind and memory. Whatever they had left me with still administers that memory.

When I examine my childhood more closely I begin to see tiny leaks left by those who should not have been there. Perhaps I was never as lonely as I profess because I always suspected there were others or at least an activity of some sort that kept me occupied. It certainly explained my preoccupations with things such as magical conjuring and secret Masonic sects, all interests that had no source of influence. It was these interests and fixations that pointed to the manoeuvres of others who came into my life like scene removers of some covert play. One of those fixations was of a familiar educating system that I believed only took place at night, that I hadn't thought about in years.

It brought me to a special preoccupation that people often have who experience the alien agenda – a secret schooling. I have read of accounts where abductees believe part of their childhood had been spent partaking in a secret educational programme that wasn't anything to do with their normal schooling. It was like a night time affair that involved other children being called away to attend a type of religious or indoctrination session in an unlocated classroom. Upon recall of these sessions, the subject can never remember why they were there or what they had learned but it was always described as a secret lesson they had to attend. Quite often, the lessons learned are said to gradually release throughout periods of their life similar to the way I believe my automated memory works.

I seemed to remember something of these nocturnal lessons being like freemasonry, a repeating trait in my life. It was something more religious than school lessons but then not quite like church. My memories of those lessons are quite vague and I don't remember them continuing for long, but I suspect they took place between the ages of ten or eleven. Something happened at night that I knew was special and magical and I remembered feeling privileged to be able to attend. During this time, (1978-1979?) I remembered having this thing about the term "night school." I knew "night school" to be nothing more than classes for grown-ups to attend after their working hours, but in my mind it had more of an exotic meaning. To me it signified a magical place in the sky that grown-ups didn't know about, one where children learned how to perform magic that they couldn't use during the day. During "night school" I could do things that would astound me, feats that left me astonished that I couldn't perform all the time. I seem to remember those secret lessons as being a chance to discover yourself and what you could do rather than just receiving facts and information. There was something about this learning environment that made you hungry to learn instead of needing the endurance to apply yourself.

When the memories of these nocturnal lessons finally resurfaced, I don't remember being taken aback by the revelation. I think it's because I referred to them with the same frame of mind I had as a ten year old boy, "All children attend these special night classes…don't they?" I was also under the impression that this procedure went back hundreds of years like our Masonic rituals. As always, I tried to rationalise my thoughts of the events and did my best to compose a structured pattern as to what actually went on. My information told a very interesting but disjointed story.

Like so many of my nocturnal jaunts as a child, I remember first being fetched by someone. These were the mysterious doll-like beings that I once termed the "night children." I instinctively knew when I would have an encounter with my artificial looking escorts as there were sensations in the room and in myself that led to their appearance. When they arrived they were always there to take me somewhere. Sometimes that was in an abstract flying craft to an unknown terrain being either a volcanic area or a desert somewhere and other times it was the "night school." I never recall where the night school actually was or even entering any particular building to get there, it was more a case of appearing. When inside, I remember it being like a long hall with no particular features, just grey walls and the familiar source-less light. I sat there amongst other children (children I seemed to know) at rows of tables arranged neatly facing the front of a classroom.

There would always be a tutor at the front and sometimes a couple of others who aided them as co-tutors. I remember having different teachers both male and female but I cannot recall anything individual about them that would allow me to remember them the way we do teachers. This was because they masked themselves very much like the robed beings. They dressed similarly to the hooded "monks" I've come across and I believe they covered their faces for similar reasons—so they wouldn't frighten us. Because of this I wonder how I ever deciphered male from female in those robes.

Around the age of ten I remembered thinking how interesting those Catholic schools were, the ones that had "monks" as teachers whom the pupils addressed as "brothers". It wasn't so much envy that I had about these schools, it was more to do with the impression I had of robed monks being mystical beings with centuries of wisdom to pass down to pupils. These impressions proved to be misleading in the real world. Monks were simply monks, men who have studied and taught religion but the robed beings I had encountered were in fact brilliant and being taught by them would have made students that way too. I don't remember being in the night school long enough to have ever acquired that brilliance as I only recall a brief term there, but the presence of these teachers seemed awesome.

Not being able to properly see their faces made estimating their age also a difficult task but I imagine that they had seen far more years than the average human pensioner. I also imagine that this age had allowed their minds to reach a potential that the human mind never lives long enough to fulfil. That wisdom came across in the most intuitive way and I can now see where my early opinion of Catholic schools and their brothers came from.

There were so many children I remember seeing in those classes and I suspect their reasons for being there were as individual as mine. I seem to recall having strange looking children in the class whom I avoided. I secretly termed these peers the wolf children because of something about their faces being that bit darker as if obscured by fur or whatever. They were strange and I remember being a touch nervous of them at all times. There was never any problem with these children or any pupils because the lessons were conducted in an unnaturally cordial manner, an oddity for a class of pre-teen children. It was I believe conducted hypnotically with the pupil's minds engaged so that normal ten-year old behaviour was discharged right from the beginning.

I also remember the transfer of information being effectively delivered and not oral which doesn't really surprise me now considering things. Looking back, I think different messages were delivered to different pupils and maybe the other two co-tutors of the class assisted in that. My messages I believe were the telepathic dramas encountered on many other occasions where things were taught by demonstration. Scenes and information were transferred the way I had learned to become familiar with from an early age and I believe this familiarity became a prime reason for contact. Perhaps I had been selected mainly because of an interactive reason. It seems that these beings can use telepathy on anyone but not everybody can adapt to their psycho-dramatic programming. I always had a knack for interpreting messages by gesture and often read into emotions very easily. So often the messages conveyed through the alien mind scenario really meant something to me. This impression alone is one of intuition.

At the time, however, I found their scenarios and mind games totally obscure and so many times I would protest unreservedly that I didn't understand. Their reply was always the same; I was repeatedly told something to the effect of "In time you will understand." Perhaps now during the recall of these strange memories was the time of which they spoke.

I wasn't alone in experiencing these scenes because I remember a few of the other children from the class accompanying me. About 3 to 5 of us would often be taken somewhere (suddenly appearing there) and observe the most fantastic and lucid three-dimensional scenes. Often the scenes themselves showed incidents that would not register in the minds of ten year olds but when I think back to them, they could have been scenes from another world or other times where things are unexplainably different. The scenes were jumbled, but I will try to relay them in a coherent way from the eyes of the same ten year old:

I witnessed different realms and terrains, some of them earthly, some of them alien. One of them that sticks out in my mind was of a strange albino race, stocky oriental people with striking white hair and eyebrows. Wherever this place was, it was bustling with these people and I recall them appearing friendly, acknowledging that I was there. As always I could appear anywhere I wanted and view the scene from all angles but whatever view I chose, these beings knew of my presence. I couldn't recognise their abode but it was a bustling and commercial town or city where everyone was industrious. They were all dressed differently but none of their clothing seemed to resemble anything from our time. At a guess I would have likened their outfits to smarter looking overalls with what looked like attachments draping from the collars and sleeves. The most noticeable aspect of this place was the people with their white hair, as there isn't a race in our world that looks exactly that way. If you were to select a well-built Chinese person, and bleach their hair and eyebrows, they would appear as this race did.

I have no real understanding of why I was ever sent to this place or what I had to do there but I suspect the stay was very brief. Looking back, it was perhaps one of those lessons in exposure where one has to become initiated or familiarised with other worlds or cultures. The oriental albinos could have been our tomorrow people. Perhaps I'll never know.

Another scene I recall being whisked off to that could have represented a future or even parallel existence was one of a huge outdoor festival somewhere. I remember being shown hoards of people gathered in a field partaking in different events like a garden fete. The people themselves looked normal and dressed no different to our era but there was another race amongst them that closely resembled apes. These were beings that actually talked, walked on two legs, and appeared quite articulate. If someone had described this to me, I would have immediately thought of the "Planet of the Apes" but it wasn't really like that. This race looked and moved far closer to actual apes than Roddy McDowall's character and didn't wear clothes like the films, just their natural fur. They intermingled with the humans quite freely but I had the impression they acted as servants or assistants to them. It seemed clear that these were second-class albeit respected citizens of this society and as soon as I recalled the scene I thought about our research into the evolutionary scale. Perhaps these were the next in line to evolve from apes the way we were said to have done thousands of years ago. Although I cannot say these beings resembled Neanderthals either. Perhaps somewhere along the line we will do something to boost the development of our closest species (chimpanzees?) allowing them to become humanised. Other than that, it might have happened on its own accord and what I witnessed was the early development. Had I seen the futuristic changes of man and beast?

If it was the future I was seeing during those hidden school lessons then I must have at least glimpsed the technology of tomorrow. Over two decades have passed since I attended that bizarre school and some of the things I remember seeing have certainly not come about yet. I remember seeing aeroplanes in the sky that quadrupled the size of our own and appeared to have "twin bodies". Where we have two wings attached to the plane there were two huge carriages side by side that would have contained far more than the average jumbo jet. The wings seemed to effortlessly support these twin carriages and strangely not a sound was made as it flew.

I remember seeing a peculiar steel substance like quicksilver that would mould into any given shape and saw that there were machines made of it, too. I understood it was like an organic steel that could be grown into things governed by a type of technological gene to determine its shape and function. When I think back to other events, I seem to recall biological machines. When I try to recollect being inside that amber craft in '94 which in itself was like a mutating cell, I had a feeling that everything around me was not just technologically sophisticated but biological. The only existing machinery we can relate this to is perhaps the physical brain or maybe the complex alterations of a rain forest.

Now that I've seen these things it makes me wonder when the new breakthrough in science will take place. There have been breakthroughs in genetic science where animal clones can been created but I often wonder when and where this science will border onto the domain of the microchip and complex machines can be built biologically. Personally, I hope we're a long way off. I feel that when discovered, something hideous could come about on which only the highly developed and humane minds of an age far from now should deserve to work. The possible "techno-gene" in the hands of the primitive doesn't bear thinking about. Although I believe that biological machines are something that will come about.

So many impressions and opinions that I have harboured over the years seem to have stemmed from my attendance at that strange school. Where else would a boy of ten reared in the television age acquire the taste for stage magic, a visual art long forgotten through TV culture? I often felt I had an education coming from elsewhere and perhaps most of my strange ideas about the world during adolescence reflected that. Bizarre theories poured out into my schoolwork from that age where I could conjure up ideas straight from left field, leaving myself curious and the teachers bemused.

Around the age of 11 I remember writing an unusual essay when asked to write a piece for homework about how the future might be. I came up with an idea about a worldwide network that defended the earth from invasion (this was before I knew about President Reagan's Star Wars project). Not only did this network defend the earth but it could locate all living entities within the planet by picking up on their psyche to monitor their well-being and safety. Basically it was a worldwide x-ray able to penetrate through any matter in order to home in on anyone's energy field anywhere. At that age I didn't necessarily use terms like "psyche" or know much about people's energy fields but I described what I had in mind aptly for a boy of 10. I remember calling this network the God Ray as it was like a computerised mind that protected all its people with the presence to observe all, much like the idea of God. Today I would have translated this story more scientifically, but at the time my only references were religious or magical. Like so many of my ideas, the essay wasn't even brought up by the teachers as they were becoming wise to my odd theories. I hadn't thought about that essay or the "God Ray" in years, but recently a memory cropped up that put it back under the magnifying glass.

Something happened during my term spent at the strange school that made me realise where this God Ray originated. I seem to remember being taken by one of the hooded teachers to view something, something I wasn't to remember. I saw an image of the Earth from space, something I had seen on numerous occasions but completely forgotten about. On this occasion the whole planet was enveloped in something like a slight transparent field consistent over both hemispheres. Once again I had the dual vision where I could see the Earth with or without the field depending on which view I chose. The option to see it with the field was a deliberate move by the teacher to allow me to see its sheer vastness. I could even hear voices or thoughts of the planet's inhabitants, sounding like an orchestra, all expressing their collective joy and gratitude that this protection existed. I suspect the image and voices were induced rather than my witnessing anything real because I know how these alien masters of illusion can beguile. Whatever the scenario was, it left an immediate impression in me about the human need for a god of some kind to overlook and account for each of its billions. This, however, was not a god but a high-tech contraption that seemed to convey another message about the importance of sophistication and how it should benevolently serve mankind.

I even had the impression that the field didn't just home in on living psyche but also had a purpose for picking up spiritual energies, perhaps even for an afterlife. This brought home to me the opinion that spiritual matters weren't just the domain of religion but had a huge place also in scientific development. I have always been interested in the area where religion and science cross, thinking that there will be a time when the two work as one. This could well have been an actual scenario of the future where we are governed this way with the help of alien intervention. I have always imagined that technology and spirituality in the alien realm is actually the same.

Because of this insistence for amnesia following an alien manoeuvre I was never allowed to use their education once I had received it. The God Ray was just another unaccounted fixation in a young mind that had to wait years before the idea was given some substance. I remember that when this memory broke through I tried in vain to find that old school essay from the small collection of schoolwork that I actually kept. Nothing could be found and I certainly wouldn't have kept anything from the mysterious night school. From memory I can recall a few of the points made in that essay but it was only a vague outline of something I believe came from my imagination. Its purpose was similar to the existing Strategic Defence Initiative, to defend against enemy invasion (even if that enemy happens to be outer space) by the way of a force-field instead of satellites. It waves could pick up human aura anywhere in the world and also recognise discarnate auras as if to rescue "lost souls." I think that was the gist of it, imaginative stuff for an eleven to twelve year old. If anything like the God Ray comes into existence, it certainly won't be in my lifetime. I hope that maybe my words of it here are immortal.

There are certain traits from my experiences in the night school that have taught me much about the alien's existence. In order to understand this realm I call the Otherness, it is important to consider an existence known as Omnipotence. So far I have experienced things such as dual vision, simultaneous time, and states of being that allow the "bigger picture" to truly be seen. All of this points to a different way of existing and a transition to something very much like omnipotence. When I experienced the induced scenarios, I felt the ability to acknowledge and observe everything in the scene from any vantage point I chose. To put it another way, I felt like the all-encompassing entity with the ultimate overview similar to my childhood figment—the God Ray. This meant I could see not only different angles of the scene but the viewpoints of those partaking in it, almost as if their emotions and experiences were mine. This overview even allowed me the "timeless zone" perspective where I could see "all at once" like a birds-eye view of past, present and future. I could describe this as a multi-viewed, multi-experienced and multi-timed overlord's perspective that understood the scene like no other. You can immediately compare this state as being a god-like entity with an omni-consciousness and this brings me to the comparison of the spirit.

I think that when we die, we transform over to omnipotence and have the ability to dwell in a number of places rather than just physically exist in one. This is perhaps what is happening when we experience the haunting of a place where the spirit doesn't seem to acknowledge that it is dead and exists only in a time warp of the way it previously lived. There are often cases where a spirit seems unable to conceive the time passed since dying and behaves in a strange multi-conscious way, existing in inanimate objects (often walls) with the tendency to replay events from the past. Historical armies have been seen re-enacting famous battles from the past without an inkling that they were slain hundreds of years beforehand. Even apparitions of inanimate objects such as their guns and artillery are seen, which suggests the possibility of a replayed time warp rather than conscious spirits of the dead.

The point I want to raise here about omnipotence is that of "dwelling" and the ability to exist at a number of levels or even in different times. It's possible that our consciousness radically changes when passing over to the other side where we achieve our dwelling or god-like status and can see the overlord's picture of life and the universe. When you try to think of the afterlife in an earthly sense using our physical laws and consider it spent for eternity in a realm with everyone who has ever died and endless more that will, then paradise must in itself seem purgatory! Consciousness would have to transform tremendously for the afterlife to be imaginable.

There is evidence for this transformation because the messages that are supposed to be heard from deceased entities during séances often sound as though they come from another consciousness. So many of the supposed dead have been known to relay messages that seem incompatible with those contacting them and other spirits who are preoccupied with things that wouldn't normally be of interest to the dead. I remember reading of incidents where entities have expressed odd things like a sexual interest in those summoning them or an interest in things of importance during their lives. A communication problem is experienced during these sessions and perhaps that points to a shift in consciousness. Instead of achieving an earth-like conscious interaction with an entity, the person on this side will be baffled by the irrelevance or banality of the liaison almost as if they were talking to someone in their sleep. On this side of reality, for instance, we desperately want to learn of what actually happens after we die and perhaps on that side they might want to know why a particular horse won the derby when they lived.

That I believe is the incompatibility of entities whether they are departed humans or extraterrestrials. It seems to be when they transmute over to this side their behaviour becomes absurd. Visiting aliens have been known to do obscure things like steal children's toys and return them days later! I have come across this high strangeness which sometimes leaves me wondering if my memory is at fault, but then I have to reserve the possibility that the "child in the night school's" perspective will be different. Although after reading so many similar accounts from people who unlike myself have acquired the clarity of hypnosis that often relay both the ridiculous and cryptic, I can't really refute the theory of absurd ETs. From their reality looking out, perhaps ours is incompatible?

It isn't so much the misunderstanding of earth culture by aliens, it's probably the contrast in consciousness particularly if they are looking at our existence from the domain of omnipotence. The contrast in reality is I think where high strangeness and communication problems come from. Trying to imagine this contrast is like considering two submarines trying to make communication from different frequencies underwater. The rare transmission picked up can only be expected to be poor. Transition (humans becoming astral) also shows the teething problems of incompatibility.

I cannot forget for instance that night of the ceremony where I had been collected by such an unusual car. It was as if it came from a past that we never actually had. I remember experiencing all the high tech features such as an engine that never ignited and a soundless journey as if the car was hovering yet inside could not have been more removed. The interior resembled something I estimated came from the fifties! When applying a closer examination to incidents like these, the more imaginative investigator might come across a consistency in the inconsistencies that could explain so many peculiarities ranging from the mysterious "Men in Black" of UFOlogy to the strange habits of extraterrestrials supposedly living amongst us.

There were and still are memories resurfacing from my time in that strange school that I believe taught me things such as my experience of omnipotence. I seemed to have been taught how to experience this state of being and seeded with the knowledge of how it might work. As always, that knowledge comes to me in slow acting doses leaving me even more confused upon arrival. These days I no longer question the source of my knowledge now that I am aware of my short term spent at the "night school." The knowledge I normally have of the world reminds me how the living can also be plunged into different planes of consciousness where time is absent such as in meditation or some drug induced states. Personally I have experienced neither but the suspicion I have of these states being the preserve of the departed is an impression firmly seeded into me at an early age. I seemed to have had ideas about the dead and ethereality quite early on, most probably from that school but the way I believe I was taught these things came from demonstration. I had been allowed to experience dual vision and simultaneous time from the experiencer's point of view by becoming them for a short while. There is no better teacher than experience and in my case it had conveyed things that words couldn't. This futuristic educating technique had given me ideas about the world, some that proved to cause hardship at times and others that became the bases for some intriguing theories.

I have learned that death isn't the final veil but the first platform for a series of transitions. The first of these transitions are what so many experience during out of body/near death experiences. Many people claim to have left their physical bodies only to inhabit another, exactly the same, but astral. This body has a duplicate of all the physical features of the first—arms, legs etc but can perform the most outstanding feats such as flying or walking through walls. I remember being in this state a number of times and remember feeling humanoid in shape but I am convinced this isn't the final form. It is an in-between state that allows the soul to explore and we often hear of secret personnel adopting this form for psychic espionage when carrying out "astral projection." Perhaps this form is used for helping the deceased to acclimatise to the spirit world after dying because I am sure that, like something reptilian, this form sheds its skin to transform to yet another which isn't humanoid. Not all near death experiences (NDEs) report being physically the same when passing over, some have been reported to be spherical in shape while others insist they were just an energy field.

This in-between state that borrows most of the body's characteristics is as far as I have ventured into the other side although I could be wrong. The multi-visioned and omnipotent experiences I recall during those scenarios were very much like being a dwelling "entity" of some kind and I don't remember leaving my body. Sometimes it might even be a transition where the actual body becomes astral because even during the strange nightly jaunts of my childhood, I don't remember actually leaving a body. That night in the park which I have labelled as a classic UFO abduction, I only remember my body becoming unusually light rather than it actually leaving anything. My figure seemed to have become specially moulded to suit the task ahead where I would pass through that portal in the cell-like craft's underside just like tissue getting sucked into a vacuum cleaner.

The strange domain of the Otherness which I grew up with and often found myself plunged into the heart of is a spiritual and quantum level of higher vibration and lower density that has proved to accommodate the physical and help it adapt. I don't even have the grasp of science to begin to explain how that works but in the words of physicist and paranormal investigator Sir William Crookes, *"I didn't say it was possible, I just said it happened."*

The popular theory seems to be that if other dimensions did exist and humans had the ability to travel there, the physical frame would perish as soon as it arrived much the same way if we went outside Earth's atmosphere in our flesh. The molecular make-up of the physical is said to vibrate at light speed and should we exceed that speed, it's surmised that our body's atomic structure would rearrange, horribly so. To reach that speed and travel to this new dimension, we would first have to rearrange ourselves that way and that is exactly what I believe alien entities did to me. Without resorting to an out-of-body form, a form we can use to access an infinity of realms, my physical was altered so that I could access their world and that is ultimately what I believe alien entities to be- the physical travellers of the spirit world.

It's also believed that if they can access our reality this way but we can't get to theirs, they must be depressingly superior to us in terms of sophistication. I strongly suspect this is what they want us to believe in order to prevent mankind getting any nearer to their abode. Remember how deception seems to be a tool used to protect their aloofness and discourage anyone from getting close. It was after all the purpose for one of their pseudo-dramatic scenes imposed on me to steer my interests away from their existence – the busy street scene with the ghostly images in and around it. "Our world is immaterial, you cannot access it, look to other things…" That fuzzy message impressed upon me the perfect disincentive for wanting to investigate their agenda further.

Looking closer at what it is they try to hide, one begins to get an idea that they may not be as distantly ahead as it appears. Scientists and paranormal investigators are getting the gist that quantum physics might be the secret behind their elusiveness and judging by the slip-ups occasionally made due to this transitional "incompatibility" I spoke of, perhaps they aren't totally infallible either. Consider how this incompatibility makes them seem quite novice at times and their interactions an embarrassment. Perhaps even after 50 years or so, alien beings are still fumbling to find their way in our world like astronauts warily probing a new planet. I agree that they must be technologically advanced to a point, but in terms of interaction, we may appear as equally mysterious and disconcerting. Consider how many times humans have been said to have approached odd looking beings amidst their strange activity and upon the horror of realising that they're not human, the beings are said to react with equal horror and flee back to a nearby craft for takeoff! Also, look at the bungled attempts of alien abduction where the victims are said to have remembered everything and even managed to recover implants for inspection. My own sudden memory of the school medical room incident was just another of the hundreds of slip-ups coming to attention that point to covert involvement going on worldwide. I wasn't supposed to know what was happening. The beings couldn't have demonstrated that more convincingly.

These slip-ups and their desperate rectification point at something to our advantage and I think that we as humans deserve to exploit it. Now that a flaw can be seen in their imperviousness, abductees and other victims of the paranormal ought to open it for as much information as possible. This brings me to the work of Derrel Sims also known as the alien hunter who is famous in the U.S. for his research into the study of alien implants and the opinion of being able to "fight back". His work is viewed as controversial, but it does at least get down to the brass tacks of the alien threat and its fallibilities. It also takes away the inaccessibility of all things paranormal and explodes the taboo around these subjects even when they border on religion. This is basically the motive behind the formation of CE5, my now defunct study group—to get behind the mystery of these things and remove their appearance of distance. I believe that once uncovered, the unknown will remain known forever and I would recommend the work of the "alien hunter" to anyone exposed to the much avoided reality of the paranormal. It wouldn't just be for popularising the work and beliefs of Derrel Sims himself by fighting back it would instead enable victims to exploit the information of the alien agenda.

By trying to chronicle everything that's happened to me I am indeed milking that gap for as much information as it manages to leak. I made a concrete decision some time ago to try to compile all the disjointed information from scratch. It was a choice for personal empowerment, an option that I believe paranormal intelligences really didn't want me to explore. The preferred and easy way would have been for me to ignore everything as an involuntary fantasy and continue with my life as complacently as I had done so far. For about three docile years or more, doubts and crippled motivation had been responsible for this irrational denial of things that had blatantly manifested themselves to me by accident. My further investigation into those things revealed memories that clearly weren't accidents. These had to be compiled regardless of the negative influence left in me by the Programmers and it wasn't until sometime towards the end of 1999 that I decided to begin this.

The strangest year for me was 1996. It began with a life altering revelation and the departure of an old friend to which I had been hypnotically attached. Instead of putting pen to paper right away to record all I remembered, I was instead left in an absolute daze about what I had been involved in. Take into account that the only memories with me were of the ceremony and the psychic UFO event in the park. My period of open-mouthed astonishment made that year pass quickly, which makes me look upon this dazed feeling as the beginning of an induced spell. As months went on, memories were glowing through the haze making me realise how involved I actually was with the ethereality. I couldn't document it because everything seemed so unreal and badly sequenced. The years 1997, 1998 and 1999 were a kind of imbibing period where I slowly drank in information while being thickly amidst a strange spell. I couldn't snap out of it and was diagnosed to be suffering from an obscure depression around that time. My feelings were of chronic lethargy and being preoccupied with obscure things, making concentration impossible. I was unable to hold down a job and first applied for a disability benefit in early '97. I remembered having so much information that I wanted to share, but conditions prevented me from articulating it correctly.

There is a lot to be said for experiencing a "spell" and I had started to realise what "casting a spell" entails. This feeling I went through wasn't necessarily one of suffering, it was more like I had been "tranquillised" or deliberately subdued for my own safety. All my emotional and cognitive tendencies seemed to be especially altered to allow for the gradual "information deposits" and my reactions to them. The spell itself was a cleverly operated contrivance of something left in my mind that still feeds information to this day. I believe that spell wore off sometime towards the end of 1999, when I found the capacity to deal with the bizarre information.

So far, I had a wealth of memories that didn't belong, consisting of an astral abduction, performance of magic, strange terrains, future science and a childhood school that wasn't even my own. I seemed to be able to put that information together to form some coherent pattern or reference to something but it wasn't easy. When that spell wore off, it seemed to have been activated by something and I believe that was my acknowledgement the "night school". When I recalled that school and why I attended, the 3-year spell seemed to have miraculously lifted. I still don't know what the significance of that was, as it appeared symbolic of something to do with maturity or "passing over." Now that I knew about the secret education, perhaps I had reached a level of trust or become mature enough to deal with it.

So much was still disjointed and I wanted a way of broadcasting this information purely to see how familiar it would be in the outside world. My first move perhaps wasn't a wise one in terms of broadcast but it allowed me a chance to concisely document my story and remain anonymous. I chose to compile it all onto a web page which I felt would provide me with the immediate empowerment I desired. Telling my story on the Internet seemed an ideal choice.

The launch of the Internet took off in a big way and came to our shores commercially towards the end of '94. It was something I was immediately drawn to and went in for 100% even though I only had a passing interest in computers. It's interesting how the Internet and its functions naturally appealed to those with secret lives. I immediately saw this as a medium to tell my story.

I remember typing out an outlined narration about what I believed happened to me from my first out-of-place memory to the night of the ceremony. Because I knew this work would be anonymous, I didn't hold back on anything and felt free to tell the story like it was. I later played around with my illustrative skills and designed a background for the text together with a few pictures and a contact e-mail. I felt that something promising would be on the web soon. My finished web page was an essay on a mysterious silver backdrop just to look "new-age." At first it seemed rather long for an introductory web page but it accurately told my entire story condensed. On the other hand, maybe it was short for a lifetime's series of events. I wasted no time in uploading it and realised how rewarding online authoring could be. Here was my very own story and I had advertised it also on a few message boards from similar paranormal web sites.

The whole purpose for uploading my story this way was for it to act as bait for someone professional out there who might actually recognise what my experiences were. I was ideally hoping that a specialist in the field of paranormal studies would see my work and reply with something to the effect of "ah yes, the beings you describe were in fact..." Maybe I could contact those with similar experiences to glean information. I would acquire some answers without revealing who I actually was. Being relatively new to the Internet, there was always that disturbing notion in the back of my mind that a whiz hacker somewhere could break through my email anonymity and know who I was. Not that my story would have had any importance to anyone at this stage, it was more a case of the same old embarrassment.

The first mistake someone makes when launching their own web material for the first time is thinking that their site will be seen by the world. Potentially that's true, but people forget there are already a zillion or so similar sites for viewing that make a "web page" appear like a page from one book of thousands in a central library! The paranormal was a hot topic on the Internet and there was untold material along with mine. Nevertheless I was eager to see that if thousands could read it, one of them just one might be the person who could shed light on my mystery.

I allowed the page to be up there for a few months while I went about my daily activities still feeling the tail end of being trance-like. In this time the response I received from my disclosed email proved to be very poor. Perhaps I should have used a visitor's facility to register how much traffic actually came to the page but I had no knowledge of those tools then. The ones that bothered to respond by email were not the sort of people I had hoped to connect with anyway. The replies were few and far between asking the occasional banality like what planet the aliens came from and how I should first get in touch with my "inner" self. Following that there were the volley of infuriating sales adverts asking to place their banners on my site, the kind which cause delete keys to lodge. Unless I advertised my site right under someone's nose, there world almost be no replies of a non-commercial nature.

This was no terrible disappointment because I at least embarked on my first attempt to write about these experiences and given that they were not unpleasant, it wasn't a difficult task. The benefit of this was that I was now able to see the pattern of where my life had gone with interaction and the ludicrousness wasn't as ludicrous once I saw it in writing. I realised it simply told the story of a person experiencing something outside their normal sphere of activity and daring to define it. I kept the written work I had made but finally withdrew the web page after having it on-line for the few non-productive months.

Months had passed and I began to realise that what I had written had "holes" in it. This wasn't because my story was just an outline, it was because I realised so many other things had taken place that I was just starting to remember. Memories of events were continuing to surface and it felt that so much of what I put together needed rewriting. Some of the hazy events that I knew about were starting to get properly explained while others seemed totally new! This was the beginning of a confusing period of falsehoods and rewrites. It felt like I was regularly coming across these peepholes that enabled me to see things that bit clearer and each time I did, things needed to be added or altered. I cannot say when I will see the ultimate picture because those peephole memories still resurface. What I can say is that towards the end of 1999, my strange spell of obliviousness wore off and the picture seemed more reliable than it had ever been.

My most recent revelation, the "night school" was perhaps the ultimate bombshell that turned everything my essay told upside down. All that had happened during my personal history of interaction and the beliefs that I insist stemmed from it had to be reconsidered. It seemed that what I had learned during that secret education of my childhood was the cornerstone for so many of the ideas I had about the world. The monk magicians, the magic they performed and the way they taught through demonstrative interaction didn't truly occur to me until the autumn of '99, years after the secret schooling actually took place. I remember feeling awestruck by this memory and making a definite pledge to write more than just an essay. That autumn felt like a re-awakening for me because the spell of sluggishness was going and I believed at the time that a total recall of memory was looming. The spell and how it was ever cast remains a mystery but my assumption of the total recall was incorrect. The total recall is something that still slowly unfolds but maybe that particular time was a breakthrough. I felt a sudden clearing in my life and wanted to write.

The end of '99 signified a special turning point. Added to all the millennial build up and the new century ahead came the lifting of a personal fog that had been clouding me for over three years. I suddenly felt collective and vibrant as though a deliberate restraint on my psyche had finally decided to let go. It was the long-awaited permission to write and I knew exactly how I was going to go about it. Millennium Night, as it will be remembered for decades, wasn't particularly memorable for me celebratory-wise but I will never forget my new year's resolution that night. I was going to write a book titled "The Otherness" that would tell the true story of my life's interaction with a ghostly and alien environment. The "Otherness" pretty much summed up that environment because it was a landscape of strangeness that I had been plunging into since childhood, one that had alien characteristics and proved to be not just an otherness of reality but of my consciousness. I didn't hesitate with the title as it was so fitting of everything that happened. My new year's resolution was made and clearly devised that night.

Year 2000 always sounded futuristic and even years before this date there would be the unsurprising millennial prophets who foretold the changes both calamitous and utopian for that year. In the back of my mind I had hoped that the high strangeness secretly happening in my life and untold others world finally reveal itself worldwide in a major prophetic revelation. Nothing could have been more mundanely unlike that. Jesus never made his staggering second coming and the doomsday asteroid was nowhere to be seen, and by the same token nothing was properly revealed about the secret life I had led. There were the fragments of memory resurfacing about things I didn't quite understand but there was nothing and still is nothing in the way of a "revisit" from the Programmer friends.

What I did was write about all that I remembered and even now as I write, after pages of reflective content I still feel there is a problem in terms of volume. There really wasn't enough that happened in my life to truly justify a book and being in my early 30s I feel that maybe my saga is far from over. The total recall won't be complete until a much, much later stage. I already feel that I have perhaps told my story at a premature time in life and maybe my fifty-year old self will offer a better one. Perhaps by that time there could have been this revisit from my interactors and perhaps the world might even be better equipped paranormally to deal with such a tale. Nevertheless I have conveyed the essential theme of what's happened so far and fleshed that out the best I could my theories. In terms of actual happenings, my entire saga could be written in a few pages but I think it's fairer to offer more. In order to convey such peculiarity it really needs to be accompanied by some form of sober diagnosis even if that diagnosis it is just based on opinion.

The story I am trying to tell is not an easy one, given that I am writing from the perception of another reality and an ever-growing memory recall. However, I believe in telling it like it is and it can come straight from leftfield. I could only write from my own sane interpretation and that wasn't a problem apart from the disjointedness of the facts and the incompleteness. I had taken to writing as soon as I attempted to be both honest and explanatory in delivering this saga.

I also have to accept that what I have written is not necessarily the final word on my experiences. It was only recently, after writing over 80 pages that another of those déjà vu type revelations came to me that I struggled to put together. It was as late as March 2001 (the latest of my recalls to date) that something occurred to me about the usual subjects of science and folklore. In the memory, I remember seeing things that resembled photographs or pictures that could be operated interactively. These pictures were upon flat paper just like photos only the images moved quite clearly as if seeing them on a TV screen. Whatever image I chose to home in on in the picture would suddenly zoom in and reveal detail. For instance I briefly remember seeing a picture of some soldiers in what looked like a war scene and when I wanted to get a better view of one of the soldiers, a kind of zoom lens homed in to him only to reveal that these troops were not even human. That war picture was the only photo I actually remember amongst the ones I had been given but it was a striking memory. The photos immediately reminded me of the peculiar viewing device I had been given in the incident of the school medical room where it was holographic, interactive and dependent on movement.

I didn't manage to catch any further detail of the "photos" memory but I remember another which showed a ceremony of some kind involving pixies. I think this memory came from a trigger when reading something about the Shakespeare play A Midsummer Night's Dream. There was something about the pointed hats worn by the elves or whatever they were attending the classic ceremony that immediately reminded me of something I had seen before. I distinctly remember something from my past either partaking or watching an outdoor woodland ceremony that definitely involved smaller beings like pixies wearing hats similar to that which I read about. Pointed hats are immensely significant to something both in folklore and paranormal science only I cannot remember exactly what. It could be something traditionally regimental or even practical, but the way in which these memories materialise, I'm convinced there will come a time where I will have the answer.

Rather than furiously try to slot these new recollections into what I had already written, I decided to add them as they occurred. It will demonstrate how difficult sequence can be in the occurrence of an ethereality. Perhaps I will never stop writing until the day of total recall, a day a long while from now.

It is mid April of 2001 and as I bring this saga to a close I cannot believe how many questions remain unanswered. All of my life I have been involved in something of staggering complexity and for the last 5 years that something mysteriously vanished. What should this do to an avowed sane human being without any original briefing of what the paranormal actually was? The truth is that nobody is ever really ready for when the bolt from the other side first strikes. It could be something that is meticulously planned right from the start off by a paranormal intelligence and nothing we learn truly prepares us for it. I have a personal quote for this impact: Nothing prepares you for anything alien other than something alien.

My unprepared plunge into the paranormal had never left me traumatised or even distressed, but it does seem to have left its mark on me in some intangible way. My cognition and movements appear different and lack the fluidity that other peoples' seem to have. I always feel an excess of nervous energy causing my movements to appear as jolts, something that scares the life out of horses! Also if there is such thing as IQ or at least a learning capacity then it is nowhere near the way it once was, the time when my interactors decided I needed to look elsewhere for inspiration. I cannot seem to pick up from the time during that academic flutter I experienced after my experience in the park late 1994. Concentration is more of a problem these days, and I feel that the spell I had been put under left a lasting side effect that hinders my ability to gather and coordinate thoughts. This has proved to be a problem both in the workplace and in study, but I am assuming that this restrictive barrier is only the residue of a spell once cast and perhaps a motivated concentration is the way to break through it. My choice to write is perhaps a wise one.

Other effects left over from my experiences appear to be psychic in nature although very unrefined. There are still times when I find my presence affects electrical objects such as the radio or TV and that light objects are occasionally magnetised to me, all feats that I fail miserably to conjure deliberately. I also seem to have an intuition of people and their emotions by mutually experiencing part of their psyche and sometimes their dreams.

Understandably this could put pressure on both myself close family or in a worse scenario cause me to become a likely volunteer or psychic lab rat for the fanatics that are sometimes drawn to this science. I don't want this to happen, but more importantly I desperately need to protect myself from the things that disclosing such claims can cause. I need anonymity and therefore certain details and facts in this story have been altered to protect my identity. My name is not well known and will suffice if it guarantees the safety of my own immediate sphere of affairs and those closest to me. Those people are not even aware of my double life.

The beauty of my story is that it cannot endanger anybody's lives or their careers. Interaction is a very personal thing that doesn't often go beyond the person involved and I can assure that my identity is irrelevant. I am neither a scientist nor government official and I doubt I am known that well beyond my street.

I seek to avoid the personal disruption that even a short burst of publicity sometimes causes. On the other hand I desperately want to relay my story and my purpose for writing is primarily to touch upon a familiar note with those who know what I'm talking about. I need to establish that it isn't just a subjective illusion that needs avoiding. The things that I once came across are perennial and have been secretly known about by our ancestors.

However, I feel I will be relatively safe because the majority of people will not believe a single word I have said. That is fine because in a way I really can't blame them. The interactive side of the paranormal puts the experiencer in a very difficult position leaving them as I am without a single shred of evidence or a witness to support the claims. That of course will motivate the sceptics and sadly leave the genuine subjects frustrated by their absence of evidential "legs". Although I sympathise profusely with this frustration and would champion it 100%, I really don't feel that way personally. My only request to those who don't believe me is this: just consider where it actually is that these experiences are supposed to have happened. Have they ever taken place in the reality you know? Can you bring back a sample from a bizarre dream or sudden déjà vu to prove that it actually happened?

Whatever power of convincing it takes to win over the overwhelming factor of doubt isn't something I can afford to waste my energy on. Even though I understand the doubts coming from the majority, I haven't written this book to try to win them over in any way. My aim is to strike a chord with the small minority that this has happened to and to establish with them that these things are real. Only then will the esoteric things I describe get the investigation for which they are waiting.

I want the traditions of folklore and religion to be looked into with the same seriousness that science has and for all the areas of the paranormal to be examined alongside it. It will mean getting closer to the things that we consider taboo, which is more or less what my old study group aimed to do by "getting that bit closer". The phenomena that I have experienced suggest much about an afterlife and often hint at the mysticism of religion. The sacrilege behind these subjects shouldn't bar them from getting the same scrutiny that UFOs do because I feel that one day the discovery of all these things will have been made. Feeding from the tree of life for knowledge will not be seen as a temptation by serpents forever and if the secret of the universe and the afterlife won't get unveiled in our lifetime, then it might be in our children's.

I, for one, would like to see these discoveries made, not just for an explanation into my own experiences but for the unity of both science and spirituality. As humans we will always find ourselves clawing at the boundaries of reality and our awareness won't allow us to find any last word on knowledge. That is, of course, unless we lift the boundary uncovering our "final frontiers." Achieving enlightenment of the highest level and a consciousness that answers all our questions so that we never want more—transformation to a state of omnipotence. When that revelation is eventually met by whatever means, God will be looking right back at us, with a smile.

The World

I saw eternity the other night

Like a great ring of pure and endless light,

All calm, as it was bright,

And round beneath it, time in hours, days, years

Driven by the spheres

Like a vast shadow moved, in which the world

And all her train were hurled....

Henry Vaughn (1621 – 95)

6

Aftermath:

The new revelations

The high strangeness in my life was never destined to end just because of the completion of a book. That was perhaps my safest bet and one which proved disappointingly accurate.

It wasn't long after I had put the finishing touches on my work, convinced I had covered every aspect of the interaction that further fragments of its strangeness rose to the surface. These fragments were only occasional and gradual, arriving as always in the form of dreams and obscure recollections. I didn't even have to worry about tainting these memories with imagination, as they seemed to hold their own quite vividly.

It would have been a painstaking task to jot down every new memory or suspicion trying to decipher what actually happened next to what didn't and even more frustrating to disrupt my book. So I decided to chronicle any new information within an afterword, hoping it wouldn't re-write anything I have experienced so far.

The immediate period following the completion of my work seemed a strange one. Instead of feeling the great sense of accomplishment by having addressed this obscure life of interaction I felt in a kind of limbo. I hadn't really answered the questions that I and everyone else ultimately wanted to know but instead pointed to a vague time in the future, a dismissive tactic used by so many "contactees", something that I really didn't want to do. I had after all written about my experiences in the understanding that they might conclude with an ongoing memory recall and that really leaves it as an open case for today and for many years to come.

I was left with a 90-something page testimony that people were immediately going to see as the product of a hallucinatory illness and when I read over the esotericism of what I am actually claiming, all due to the unimaginable sophistication of paranormal entities, I too would see it that way. I can only insist that I have never hallucinated in my life and that my relays are from nowhere other than personal experience. I once remember the well chosen words of a war correspondent coming back from a crisis in the Middle East who had no biased knowledge of the conflicts there – "All I saw was how it happened and I cannot be any less vague."

This lack of reference to things commonly reported before really seems to have left me without the assistance of evidence, witness or even a substantiating story. If it had not been for my knowledge of High Strangeness and the Oz Factor, I would not have put a word of this into writing and maybe decided upon psychiatry after all. Now that I read back over what I've written I begin to see the tangibility in some of the intangible things described. Maybe it isn't possible to actually bring you into the realm of a dream but I can at least try to tell you how it might work.

My original reason for defining these things was to try to connect with a tiny minority of paranormal experiencers that have had these interactive psycho-dramatic episodes in order for them to say "Hey, there really is something in what you've come across."

As my story developed, I realised I could do more than just that. What I have described could perhaps open up and establish a less-talked-about angle in UFOlogy. I don't intend to win over the majority who will understandably doubt my story but at least I might help make concrete the psycho-astral side of the phenomena for later generations to consider.

None of this actually helped; it just left me pondering in the indecisive limbo at the time. The outcome had made it difficult to put a full stop on this saga knowing that the full stop could never be accurately positioned. Not a week would go by where I didn't feel the strange sensation that more of the puzzle was surfacing thus more of the saga had to be added or re-written. I didn't feel old enough to have harboured such a mysterious past with chunks that didn't look like my own. There were times when it made me wonder whether I had been jumping in and out of other people's lives from other dimensions because the recollections didn't often appear to be from the past I knew.

It wasn't long after the time I believed I had completed my book that I read about something in the newspaper that had always fascinated me; the relationship between man and ape. An unidentified animal had been reported somewhere in the world (an interesting phenomenon related to UFOlogy where creatures are witnessed as being either unclassified or ridiculously out of place) that brought about the topic of evolution and genetics. A "man-monkey" was said to have been spotted by a number of people in Delhi India, an animal that had no reason to have been there or even in existence. Theorists were saying that it could have been a deformed ape or even the result of a freakish crossbreed but what interested the media most wasn't so much validity of the story but the way it touched upon the subject of evolution and what scientists are always looking to do to speed it up. In other words, could this be an evolvement of apes or what can possibly be achieved through science—an inevitable "man-monkey?" Let's not forget that one of the most controversial photographs taken of an alleged alien being was known as the "monkey man" in Mexico back in 1949. Flying discs were spotted over Monument Valley that appeared to be discharging small cylinders over Mexico City, one of them containing the live, three foot tall being in question. The black and white photo showed the small creature, oddly dressed in European clothing, being led away by two men presumably the authorities. For years this snapshot was unanimously branded a hoax, which it could well have been but the fact that this creature was likened to a monkey still interests me a great deal.

I have always had a thing about humanised and intelligent apes, believing I had seen them somewhere either from my blurred past of from a deeper realm of forgotten dreams. I seem to remember apes that talked quite articulately, walking around on two legs and, more intriguingly, I was not being surprised by their presence as though I was used to seeing them.

I tend to think of these memories as being from my actual past rather than a "Quantum Leap"-type slip into another person because when I think of my presence in these memories, I am often looking "up" at the beasts the way a small child would. Perhaps they were no taller than the average human and they didn't seem to pay much attention to my presence yet they would occasionally refer to me affectionately the way a passing adult might to a child. That tells me a great deal about the ages at which these memories might have taken place.

When I read this article about the unusual creatures sighted in Delhi, the written words "monkey-man" or "man-beast" seemed to ring a particularly loud bell, conjuring up many memories about the ape people. Those were the words used in the scenarios I remember, "Try to avoid the "man-beasts', they're quite harmless but best left alone." "The monkey-man is there, waiting to develop, please allow them to." I found this fascinating as I must have remembered them existing as a type of intelligent livestock. I vaguely recall overhearing these comments or perhaps being personally briefed on what they were. I never consciously remembered them this way as I only dismissed that memory as another disjointed dream but now I really felt there was a story behind the man-beast. I often felt a chill once I recapped those memories because, as primitive as the apes looked, they could talk. Just imagine having sudden memory about your dog being able to talk and it will throw everything you know about evolution out the window. This new memory was as enlightening as it was disturbing. Somewhere in my life I had seen apes that could walk and talk like people.

Other times when I believe to have seen these creatures were times when they (and everyone else in the scene) were totally oblivious to my presence. During these times I existed just as the familiar "viewpoint" where I could view scenes at any angle I chose, like the multi-perceptive omnipotence of which I spoke. All sorts of scenes were played where I could see the man-monkeys happily interacting with humans. As I suspected before, the talking apes were a type of respected manservant; they were either discovered or developed to carry out tasks. I remember seeing what we would interpret as garden fetes going on where the humanised apes would happily liaise with human masters without any animosity between them. Some apes appeared to live wild in the woodland areas where they would cling together as clans or families watching in on the strange activity of humans and developed apes. I got the impression that even the wild apes were intelligent to a point, some capable of speech, some not. I just remember them existing in a sad and inert state where they couldn't seem to decide what they actually were. They simply hung around in these clans, sluggishly brooding as though they were waiting to be developed. It was like a type of school.

What I could never work out was whether these scenes were images of the future or something quite tasteless going on now in a secret genetic farm somewhere. There is no evidence to suggest that this research or "monkey schooling" is going on anywhere but the ideas have certainly crossed people's minds over the years. "Planet of the Apes", a television series I loved watching as a youngster was based on the next stage of evolvement for monkeys and how they lived among humanity, some films showed them actually being the masters. I cannot even say it was that which influenced my visions of the ape-people, because these beasts I saw were physically far closer to their ape origins than the refined look of the actors who played them. Physically, these creatures were apes with their full body fur and no need for clothing, it was only their minds which made them appear human. I never forget the documentaries seen occasionally that demonstrate the communicative skill of apes showing them being able to select things on computer screens and the theory expressed that it is only the shape of their mouths that prevent them from speaking. If any creature could be upgraded this way it would be apes. I wouldn't be surprised to see a breakthrough of this within the next 20 years. What I saw in this cryptic way seemed incredible and disgusting. In hindsight, it was only the lack of malevolence I witnessed in the scenes that helped me warm to what I saw.

The "monkey-man" is one of those fixations that never properly wore off. Even as I read over what I originally said about their presence I feel the shiver of familiarity as though there were so much more. I honestly believe that something substantial took place in my past to which I had been accidentally exposed, something that reflects a small part of a reality that only a few people know of today. My reason for writing this book is as much to request answers as it is to reflect them. I sincerely hope that someone out there can tell me some more about the monkey-man among hundreds of other things that hang in question.

Like every other subsequent feeling or memory I had after writing the book, I couldn't afford to delve into it any further. I had re-visited all the strange places I believe I went to and retraced every unexplained step I made, only to find the same cold physical world of everyday life. It was time to take my pages of personal testimony to a publisher and it had to be one that would be sensitive to these peculiar claims without just looking for sensation. I knew this was going to have an element of embarrassment and so many times I was tempted to add or take away bits just to smother the edge off the absurdity. Had I chosen to deviate from the story in any way, the chances are the discrepancies would leak and a sharp mind somewhere would home right in on it. I also knew quite early on in my writing that it wasn't going to stretch to the average two hundred and something page epic because there simply wasn't that much to tell. A compilation of experiences, memories and some personal theories to support them would, I estimate, be around 90 pages or more, but for me that was adequate; it was the actual story.

For a first time writer, my bombshell saga and its outlandish claims were going to make it difficult to approach anyone reputable. I needed anonymity. As a particularly private person who preferred anonymity in most communication, the Internet became a natural choice and it wasn't long before I came across the world of "e-publishing." This seemed like an opening for a first-time author especially one who felt somewhat uncertain about the categorisation of his story. Anonymity was easy over the Internet and an e-publisher that I eventually contacted was very respectful of this. The good thing was that as esoteric as my experiences were, they were not likely to frighten people or put anyone's lives or livelihood at risk. The controversy factor was nil and I consider that to be a unique blessing considering what God only knows I had been in contact with.

When I first approached, someone I thought it to be more in my interests not to make an issue over this "on-going memory recall" because I had a feeling they would lose interest or say, "Come back when you're fully remembered." I may indeed have a much fuller story later on in my life but I think the time to break this news was the time after my Interactors had given me the capacity to do so, the time after their abandonment.

Even then, this capacity I speak of had its drawbacks. I remembered things and I could write about them but for most of my life my mind had been influenced by an invisible mechanism that governed my thoughts and before these beings departed, they took that with them. I had to learn to manage my mind without control and, like everything else, if you've been used to crutches it will feel strange walking without them. I had been offered new perimeters in my mind, but I found exploring them to be taxing task. Writing my story from a slow blooming memory left me unaccountably exhausted but I found the completion of this self-appointed goal delightful.

I was a new person because revelations had been made to me. Maybe I wasn't who I thought I was but I had been left to explore a new identity and sometimes that could be a draining experience. Lifelong interests had to be replaced because of these revelations, which perhaps was more educating than taxing. It would seem that I had lost my fascination for stage magic simply because the science behind it had at last been revealed. My childhood figments of wizards and "magic monks" were now replaced by alien beings because it seemed that they were my life's true illusionists.

Even with the bombshell of new knowledge, life had to go on. I felt like a patient awaiting the results of a strange new diagnosis and that its verdict wouldn't really be known until years later. The limbo state that all this had left me in meant I was too exhausted from interaction and its realisation to care. This had taken its toll on my health and everyday life and it was shocking to learn how long it was since I had actually worked. A doctor had long ago advised me to apply for health benefits after diagnosing me with a rare depressive illness related to M.E. That diagnosis was an educated shot in the dark considering he didn't know a thing about my experiences.

With everything in mind and nothing to move on to I decided it was time for a change of lifestyle or maybe a long holiday somewhere. An opportunity had arisen for me to go abroad and learn a language if I wanted and I honestly couldn't think of a reason why not. The place where the opening had been offered was in Rome Italy on a 12 week language course to learn the lingo and spend some time around the country. It was a marvellous opportunity to come across and perhaps couldn't have happened at a better time. My first concern was being able to apply concentration again given that my mind was still fragile and buzzing with activity fresh from the recent developments. I wondered how my mind would cope focusing on something else like a new language but it would be interesting to try.

They say that going away doesn't necessarily solve problems as you only take them with you but in all honesty I left on the note that they were no longer there. My demons had literally left me and in any case I seemed to have exorcised their significance by writing. The only mark they had left on my abandoned mind was a slow acting recall of memory but I found that more exciting than intruding. It had only been about the first week into my holiday that a new memory emerged.

As always I point to the great significance in "drifting-off to sleep" because I believe this hypnotic stage is uncannily receptive to all wavelengths inside and out. One evening after retiring to my room between 10:30 to 11 p.m., I lay in bed awake generally wondering about things as I normally do. That particular night I remember desiring answers to things imagining them to materialise in a way that could only be wishful thinking. "Wouldn't it be nice if someone could pop answers into my mind as I slept" was the gist of my thought but if that had been interpreted as an actual request then I wouldn't have been surprised by what I came across the very next day. That following afternoon, without warning it felt like cold water had suddenly been thrown right in my face. How did I ever manage to forget that mystical garden with all the lakes and strange seals everywhere? That seemed like years ago, so long I had actually forgotten. That was where I saw so much magic performed.

It was a distant memory of either a huge garden somewhere or a national park or woodland. The sunshine seemed to have been at its peak but I don't even remember feeling hot. There were hundreds of people around but I don't remember much about them other than they wore robes similar to the ones Asians wear and they bathed in the nearby lakes. What fascinated me about this scene were those animals everywhere that resembled sea-lions even though I knew they weren't. These creatures seemed tranquil with a placid intelligence with which I actually believe I communicated. It is because words were not spoken yet everything was immediately understood that I have to refer to telepathy once again. There was peacefulness about this communication and I seem to remember conversing with a number of these creatures, about what I'll never know. I recall seeing them scattered everywhere, some in the lakes and others resting by the banks just like seals do. They were black in colour and moved about mainly on their underside so I wonder if my prior or later knowledge of seals perhaps distorted my mind into seeing them that way. It looked as though the humans in the scene cohabited quite happily with these creatures and I got the impression that this was a type of gathering for rest rather than any mutual coercion.

Another interesting aspect was that there was something else, something alive above us overlooking the scene only I couldn't see what. That seemed to have been the extent of my memory, a frustrating boundary which I always run into during these recollections.

As always, I was overwhelmed when the new memory dawned upon me and dumbstruck when it finished. I had witnessed yet another déjà vu fade into nowhere and there was nothing I could do. This particular recollection however was interesting because it had striking similarities to the previous. The outdoor activity was there, like a garden fete where wise animals were present communicating with me, this time telepathically. Rather than humanised apes of the last memory it was seals with advanced minds. Humans were again present but I didn't pay much attention to them owing to these nondescript creatures everywhere.

What made this memory fascinating was that I seemed to have requested it as I had gone to bed the previous night thinking, "Wouldn't it be great if—" I could have put this down to coincidence, thinking that a new memory might have been due anyway, but then I once remember reading about something like this. I used to follow the case of Ed Walter's Gulf Breeze Sightings quite fanatically at one time, reading books on the subject whenever they came out even noting how his photographs of the UFO's sighted near his home in Florida were very similar to the cathedral-like ones I once dreamt about even though I suspect that was flashback. In his book, UFO Encounters at Gulf Breeze he describes a theory similar to "sleeping on it" a phenomenon where one could go to bed and request something just before dropping off to sleep and by morning either subconsciously or paranormally the answers will be there waiting. He went on to describe how a number of questions were answered this way, perhaps by forces unknown.

I have often drifted off into sleep only to be met with a string of mysterious numbers followed by lucid dreams where my answers will be cryptically demonstrated. Whether I cared to remember them the following day is another matter as more times than not dreams are commonly forgotten. It is hard to say whether these messages are generated from the subconscious or something outside but on this occasion it had seemed symbolic of something that might have gleaned answers. A mysterious park full of peaceful looking lakes where I could converse with the most tranquil creatures, could this have been one of those out-of-body experiences where I found myself in a type of Biblical Eden on the other side? Maybe that was where all my answers lay, the ones I flippantly asked for the previous night. I must admit that if it was the result that I had been looking for then I found the whole outcome very disconcerting. I could have practiced the whole sleep on it technique every other night and gleaned answers that nobody would dream of but to be honest I was too nervous. We are always warned to be careful what we wish for and I found the whole simplicity behind that accident quite disturbing. I might not want to look to deep into the esoteric in fear of what I might find and, needless to say, I didn't practice that trick anymore to this day. However, it wasn't the last I would remember about that strange garden, something I will explain later.

It wasn't the first time that an explosion of new memories had thrown everything into disarray and I don't suppose it will be the last. From experience I have found it is best to file away these memories as unsolved until another day because you get nowhere turning your mind inside out trying to understand. The memories were interesting and immensely significant but I had a life to lead.

There were physiological differences left in me as well as mental ones ever since the beings had departed. I seemed to be carrying around this excess electricity that felt particularly vibrant at times and so often I would experience an unusual static from objects and a strong effect on electrical devices. While in Italy I shared an apartment with other foreign guests who were becoming very aware of my effects on the apartment's TV. It got to the point where I avoided getting up to leave the room as the television's electrical currents seemed to follow me. I noticed that times when I wasn't expecting it, the picture would move in any direction I moved as if a magnet were being waved across the screen. Yet on other occasions whilst on my own when I deliberately tried to cause the effect nothing would happen. I tried waving my hands all over the set and even concentrating but I never could repeat the occurrence. This would happen unexpectedly with the radio, light bulbs and even physical movement of pieces of paper. Whatever static the average person was said to generate, I seemed to quadruple and spread when I least wanted to.

It is a good thing that people these days generally seem light-hearted about unusual tendencies and won't necessarily want to burn you at the stake for possessing witchcraft. During my language course, there were many occasions where each member of the class would take turns speaking into a cassette recorder. Every time it came round to me the device would either malfunction electrically or at least appear to work and then fail upon playback. It can be a touch embarrassing anyway for students having to listen to their voices in turn attempting to speak the language but when it came to mine, an unearthly static could be heard over the cassette player and my voice wasn't even audible! After a number of occasions, people's initial humour began to fade as though they were starting to suspect that perhaps I was a witch, but I quickly developed a tactic. I thought that the effect would never happen if I tried to induce it deliberately so in future I tried to be aware and actually make it happen. It worked! I had actually managed to trick the "living programme" the beings had left me with by asking it to do what I knew it wouldn't. It made me realise once more that the alien technologies were not as impervious as they appeared and had their flaws just like the average machine has. It also brought home my earlier theory of the artificial yet conscious entity within because it seemed to have an awareness manifesting in the mind or physically. When I developed this defence strategy it made me wonder if there would ever be a day where I could "talk" to the entity the same way a hypnotist can train a patient to communicate with their subconscious. Only time and an understanding of its mechanisms will tell.

Weeks had passed since the two recent phenomena and I had become involved enough in the holiday to actually put them out of my mind. That was until another bombshell was to erupt without warning that seemed to add credence to a previous one.

It started one evening after having a meal out at a Chinese restaurant and waiting to pay the bill at the cash till when I noticed a painting on the wall across the bar. It looked like one of those Hindu paintings of a vast garden somewhere with Asian-dressed beings enjoying whatever activity it was. Then something occurred to me, why were they all blue? In fact they are always blue-skinned in Hindu illustrations and I wondered why that fascinated me so. The same shiver of familiarity came over me again as I thought about that memory of the garden-like woodland area with the wise seals and the robed or sari-clad beings. They were not entirely human, either, and their skin resembled that strange cobalt colour just like those in the painting.

So much of that memory came flooding back to me that I would have struggled to remember beforehand. The people in the scene I remember were both male and female but had alien features, probably not alien compared with what would normally be considered alien but too strange to exist anywhere in our world, other than those paintings of course. Eventually when I returned from this holiday, I spent a lot of time in the library investigating Hindu art to explain where the "blue people" actually came from but so far nothing had been gleaned. Even the mysterious "grey" aliens reported today are sometimes seen as blue but these people

I saw in the memory were almost human except for that artificial looking skin.

Once I had seen that painting and just briefly wondered about its significance was exactly when the memories flooded. That alone seemed a phenomenon as it appeared to be another of those subconscious requests. That was when I remember clusters of the blue beings just gathering socially by the lakes. The seals in the scene were also scattered around just living in independent harmony with these humans like they were regular bathing guests. I cannot remember a sequence of events in this scene but it seemed like I had been conversing with the seal creatures for a while before I became aware of a presence overhead. To my amazement that presence turned out to be a ball of brilliant white light hovering above us giving off the same fiery effect of a sparkler. It made no sound as it flew over us and gently lowered to a nearby bank by one of the lakes. What happened next was unbelievable. It silently lowered more of the seal creatures from its underside onto the grassy bank. I watched them effortlessly flop down onto the floor below from an exit in this globe that I couldn't actually see almost like the craft had spewed them out. The seals were awake and active soon as they hit the floor and seemed to go in all directions.

Once the craft had done this I watched it swerve in sophisticated motion without a sound and depart the way it appeared, straight over my head and off into nowhere. For me a fantastic transpiration had just been carried out which I suspect was just an everyday task in this strange world. It couldn't have looked more alien in my eyes especially now in the recollection of a sober and unaltered mind. A ball of light delivering a pack of seals to a strange river bank surrounded by what appeared to be Hindus. What did any of this mean? Furthermore why was I being shown it? I couldn't even translate any significance to what I remembered wondered if that was my young self in the scene or the body of another I inhabited. It even crosses my mind that because these scenes are so seemingly irrelevant that I may have plunged into them by accident almost like someone walking right into the middle of a circus and was speechless by what they saw.

After I had returned home I had looked up a number of references to the paintings I first saw that triggered that memory. There were quite a few of those paintings around that depicted similar scenes and I gather them to be significant to Indian religious folk bathing in sacred rivers like the Ganges. Nearly all the Hindu art I had looked up depicted the blue beings, some with women possessing four arms or more and interestingly some nondescript creatures like multi-headed serpents. Nothing however pointed to the significance of wise-seals. I even noticed occasional bright objects in the paintings that could either have represented the Sun or strange stars but nothing like the Biblical yet technological object that hovered overhead like the classic UFO. Once again I write this book as much in request for answers as I try to offer them and I hope that my experiences will perhaps arouse someone proficient enough in Hindu folklore to point to what I might have seen.

Naturally I was rocked by this new memory just like the others, but realised how my new approach to "shelve and not to try to understand" was perhaps the best one. An open case is how that and everything else in this book remains.

"Triggers" had proved to be my most promising fuse to ignite these hidden memories. Without that painting I might never have realised the memory of the Hindu garden. I wondered if these triggers posed a threat such as accidents or unforeseen flaws that upset or even quickened the alien's programme. For instance, that memory might not have been due to release itself into my consciousness until years later perhaps. By fate I come across it much sooner. Does that mean I have tasted forbidden fruit too early? It was undoubtedly going to leave me wondering and that meant I would seek out more information continuously like a dog worrying a bone until I finally learned what it all meant. That painting wasn't the last "trigger" I was going to encounter on this holiday.

Because of my early interest in stage magic, the theatrical interest had branched out onto other areas during my younger years and onto various acts seen on the stage. The costumes and dramatic personas that appeared in drama always reminded me of something cryptic and alien. Those masks sometimes worn in plays truly fascinated me but when this theatrical interest moved onto science I never really cared to investigate the connection. It wasn't until sometime towards the end of my holiday in Rome one morning while crossing the road when I saw one of those mimes on the street corner. The connection came flooding back.

I immediately isolated this mime figure from the noise and crowds around me as I become suddenly absorbed into his/her act. It was first the pasty mask that the mime wore that gripped me, and then the solemn and demonstrative silence of their act. I had seen this figure or at least figures like it from somewhere in my past and knew it had shown me things. The familiarity was quite unnerving. It felt like someone involved was watching over me as if to say, "There, don't you remember?"

He continued to dance and act oblivious of me watching but I noticed something striking when he appeared to look right in my direction. A silent masked figure used to look at me that way when instructing me to do something. I remember how the figure would instinctively know whether or not I could carry out the given task and always knew exactly how I felt about it. The method was, as always, telepathy which I had now accepted as a basic rule of alien communication but I remembered the mime figure being particularly demonstrative and taking time to show me things.

I would have liked to have stood and watched that all day had I not had other things to do, but the other shoe dropped by the time I had reached the other end of the street. This particular event I remember having had taken place amidst my early adulthood but I'm sure I had seen the pathos on a number of occasions beforehand, right back to childhood. That masked or shrouded figure had been responsible for taking me on nightly excursions as a small boy to places I couldn't even fathom. However, the recent encounter with my entourage had suddenly become very clear.

It might have been around 1991 because I remember being in my early 20s and I seem to recall being on a trip somewhere out in a wilderness. I have often put this "trip" down to a dream because no such excursion had taken place or even been planned. The environment I had been plunged into I couldn't even identify and certainly didn't resemble anywhere on our hospitable planet. All I recall was being led by one of those theatrical mimes who said nothing but explained absolutely everything by gesture, the genius technique and why it interested me. "He" was dressed in either black or dark clothing that reminded me of stage costume and I seemed to know this individual unusually well. The terrain we were in was as equally peculiar and I wondered how I even got there given that it looked too barren and remote to be anywhere in England. All I saw was a landscape of rocks stretching for miles with nothing on the horizon but more rocks. It was impossible to see how far we had come as it was like that in all directions. Even the sky was different and appeared an artificial deep purple and like nothing we see in any of our seasons.

Where we were seemed so remote that you would have at least needed a helicopter to arrive or leave but that wasn't the case. It was just I, him and quite possibly another planet, uninhabited by the look of it. I don't remember feeling temperature or any of the harshness associated with these places but then the scenarios always appeared dream-like anyway and even when I do remember, I will often find physical proof such as blisters even though I maintain they are dreams. All I seemed to do in this scene was follow the being in front who occasionally looked behind to check on me and direct further. As I followed on his trail I couldn't help notice his dress. From behind it resembled one of those black religious missionaries outfits together with the broad rimmed hat that he wore. The only thing preventing me from thinking he was a missionary was that phantom mask on his face every time he peeped around.

I had no intention of doing anything other than follow very strictly because, from what I could see, there was no direction to anything in a place like this. I might have been in the Australian Outback or the Sahara. He looked around at me one last time as we seemed to stop. I had followed him to a tall ridge and when I reached him he gestured me to behold what was below. It seemed to be a huge, vast canyon with an immense clearing amongst it even though it looked barren. He kept holding his hand out for me to look in awe at everything below and even seemed concerned that I didn't share his enthusiasm. It was just a huge rock clearing sometimes found in the valleys of famous mountain ranges such as the Grand Canyon and apart from the unearthly sky above and the way it seemed to have no affect on the light cast on us and this terrain (which was indeed strange) I couldn't really see what I was supposed to acknowledge.

"I can't remember this place," I said to him.

A strange comment seeing that nobody was suggesting that I should. The communicative impression I got from this scene was that I was only being shown something, maybe for the first time but then who knows what subliminal messages were being relayed in this silence. He appeared to react with a slightly humorous dismay and surprise in his response and it looked as though he prepared to do something. That something could well have been the wave of a magic wand because within the blink of an eye I was in another place.

Once again I was plunged into yet another totally disorientating reality. This one I am not even sure I have the hallmarks to compare with but I would bravely attempt a guess that this was a glimpse of the future. This time I was riding through the sky in a small but totally transparent craft. Below was a night scene of a modern city into which I believe the craft was about to descend. As I experienced this preparation for landing I was greeted with fantastic glimpses of all angles of the city as this "glass bubble" lowered down into a street between rows of skyscraper-like buildings, a view as good as seeing the world from a cable pulley. The glimpses were brief but unforgettable. I gathered that everything I saw was ultra commercial and cosmopolitan; I say ultra because I couldn't recognise anything. That was until I saw the most familiar and commercial logo ever above one of the street levelled buildings, the famous letter "M" in yellow on a homely red background, the welcoming logo of McDonalds. I feel myself wince once more as I describe that and honestly wish it was something less familiar but there it was, the instantly recognisable insignia of the world's most successful fast food chain. What was totally different when the "bubble" lowered into street level was that I saw the entire boulevard taken up with the McDonalds business. Everything on that side of the street was paraded with their shop front imagery but I got the impression that it wasn't just one long restaurant. Intriguingly I was looking at what seemed to be a whole street of a multi-faceted business that could have been restaurants, hotels, stores, banks, you name it all ran by the McDonalds chain. If this was a scene from the future then I have learned something about the business of tomorrow. Rather than just sticking to fast food, a global business like this had perhaps branched out onto other services all under the same name? This is a fascinating thought considering that big business is always looking to expand and maybe on a company blueprint somewhere this concept is being planned.

This scene was brief, maybe because I interrupted it. Even though I had been deliberately induced into this scenario I remained physically being back in the rocky terrain. It was like being in one of those lucid dreams having knowledge of where you actually are and being able to purposely drift in and out. I knew it was that "dual-vision" experience again where I could observe more than one scene. Just after I had taken in the wonder around me of that strange city I had somehow snatched myself back with the being. When I think back to this ability I realise that it's like working between applications on a computer. While on the Internet you could have a number of web pages loading and easily be able to switch between them using alt + tab keys, just as I switched between these realities. It was disappointing when this happened because there were things about the city that I wanted to know: where was it and when was it? If it had been a city so many years into the future where McDonalds monopolised the entire street then why show me? Had I unwittingly asked for this information or was it deeply significant for me?

I don't remember being back for long after that scene because I had instantly "toggled" into another one. This time I found myself inside a huge and semi-dark dome. It seemed to be taller than it was broad and I found myself exploring its limits by floating upwards. I wasn't alone, either; there were hundreds of other people, as if it were a type of futuristic aviary for humans. Everybody floated around without purpose like it was a way of relaxing leisure. I noticed that some people around me used small boards for their motion which reminded me of the floats used for learner swimmers at leisure pools while others and myself free-floated. This seemed optional and might have been an equivalent to beginner and advanced. I also noticed that as I floated vertically there were levels in the walls like platforms and I couldn't see how far up or down this column went because it was either too dark or too distant. Movement didn't seem to be restricted in any way and it was exactly like the anti-gravity that astronauts use in space. That must have been what it was, a human floatation aviary for the future of relaxation. It seemed to have provided everything from platforms to hover-boards and gave the distinct impression of a leisure centre of tomorrow.

The next scene I suddenly found myself in was less leisurely and far more industrial. This time I observed from above what looked like a vast quarry in a mountain range similar to the canyon I had just witnessed. Only this time it was almost dark (no hint of the purple sky) and the activity below was littered with work staff and machinery that I couldn't identify. Upon closer inspection I noticed they were working around the most gigantically wide potholes in the ground that seemed to go down infinitely. It seemed that I had been made to observe the floating activity once again as I saw hoards of people going down into the shaft and coming back up by means of floatation. A huge operation was taking place that I could only identify as mining. Whatever the images were meant to convey to me, it made perfect sense that the anti-gravity ability was used for deep mining of minerals.

What better way could anyone have of mining than actually floating down there without the limiting need of cables or climbing equipment? I watched the miners slowly penetrate the darkness of these huge shafts and watched their white coveralls gradually diminish into the darkness below. God only knows how far that shaft went down but as soon as one or two descended, a few more rose up. The floatation was fantastic and it made me wonder how they manipulated the ascent and descent.

What I had been shown seemed to be a sneak preview of how they will mine in the future, using floatation. After it had been revealed, the same questions as to its significance returned—why show me? I am not a miner and never did discover what they actually mined.

The only connection I could make was to the vast canyon that the being originally showed me before I was zapped away on scenarios. Maybe the first was the quarry where they mined, but shown in daylight? All I could decipher was that I had been given a lesson in flotation and its uses. In some ways it made a lot of sense because if we could use anti-gravity it could be exploited for leisure as well as industry. Flotation, a way of relaxing today is used in leisure centres that have water filled tanks for people to unwind in both darkness and silence. Floating in "nothing" could be the new age way to ultimate tranquillity. What struck me some time after I encountered these scenarios was an idea I once contributed to a local magazine in a competition for a leisure pursuit of the future. This happened years after the "forgotten" floating experience and my entry was without surprise the floatadrome and the way I described it in my entry did sound like a human aviary. As soon as I remembered seeing that competition, my idea sprang to mind without really questioning its source. Just like my written ideas at school, the entry had been written off as being too obscure because I never heard anything of it. This had been just another example of the source-less ideas and strange fixation my life had become accustomed to.

I am not sure how or when that mining scenario came to an end, but I'm certain its beginning, end and complete control were centred around the pathos. I say that because his bland mask was the last thing I remembered seeing. There was yet another scene but I cannot be sure if that happened the same day or a much later one. It was so hard to decipher these scenes' sequences and how long they actually continued. Had the next one taken place on another occasion, then I really feel it must have been just days later because this batch of memories appeared closely linked both in significance and period.

Once my memory had been triggered that day by the pathos-mime on the street, I had stopped to think long and hard about these memories knowing there was yet another in the pipeline. I had made that afternoon my own, to be alone and with my new revelations knowing that after I had carefully thought and written through what I remembered, I would open my mind to the next. Like in the other scenes, the new one revealed yet more science without even hinting at its relevance.

This new scene, which I believed took place on a separate occasion to the other two, began when I found myself in a crowded place somewhere with the familiar sensation that those around me were unaware of my presence. It looked like one of those vibrant transport terminals for trains or buses where people rushed in all directions to get tickets and information with queues everywhere. This place looked unreal with a strange and exaggerated sophistication about it, a place that we wouldn't normally come across with machines everywhere that were not used in our world. They seemed to be devices that I could only interpret as projectors that emitted three-dimensional images anywhere they wanted so convincingly that I could hardly tell real from image. All of the images were of people demonstrating or explaining something. The machines themselves resembled those sophisticated biological devices I mentioned in an earlier chapter, the ones that upon appearance only resemble something odd organically grown but once activated appear to do things that our most upgraded computers cannot. They were machines that resembled pods and at the same time didn't quite look like either. All I remember seeing was that these devices were everywhere in the terminal each giving advice to people who requested it.

I remember paying too much attention to these "projectors" and their images to really take notice of the people around me, but I did notice they were dressed differently to our usual commuters. Instead of the sober business suits normally worn, they were dressed in those gowns again only they weren't Asian or even like the "blue" people I saw from that garden. Even the gowns they wore were not totally familiar as they only reflected Asian wear and some of the clothing looked outright futuristic. Just like the machinery, there were telltale signs of where they might have originated but then there were features that notably clashed. For instance, why would so many seemingly white Westerners dress like Buddhists or Hindus and if they did, why add strange futuristic headpieces or bangles that might come from a fictional space colony?

Just like the other occasions, I never really got to grips with why I was actually there, but impressions were strong. The significance of me witnessing these machines wasn't just to show me 3D projections, it was to do with an individual's ability to manifest in an apparitional way. This signified omnipotence I spoke of earlier seemed to be a major theme in my education. Apparently the people of tomorrow could transmit by manifesting just like a message does when sent electronically. The lesson I learned was multi-awareness; I could perceive the scene without physically being there and witnessed others who could appear through these machines. For the first time, this might have been a test as well as a lesson. The pathos being, the instigator of this scene was testing my ability to get noticed. I am not sure what it actually was that I was supposed to do to get noticed because all I possessed was this multi-perceptive view without even a physical form. My impression was that I was supposed to appear the way those other people did from the machine. I couldn't.

The scene instantly shifted to another; this time I was on a train. The train's interior was not particularly future looking, but what appeared unusual was that apparitions would appear and the passengers barely took notice. They would suddenly appear next to someone to pass on a message of some kind and then vanish. It was as occasional as someone's mobile phone ringing and that was the level of normality of which it seemed. But still, neither the apparitions nor the people knew I was there, whatever the entity "I" actually meant here.

That was it. I couldn't seem to manifest that way, so perhaps I had failed my test but it was where the scene ended and I was back with the pathos. Again I was with my guide in the rocky terrain with its strange purple sky. For the first time, he seemed understanding and even hinted humour so maybe my "test" wasn't that much of a disappointment. Again, no words were spoken but I was gestured to follow him. This time it seemed to be the way back (over the rocks that I believe I clambered over days previous). He effortlessly led from yards in front as I followed in his trail. I feared that I might lose him as he strode ahead almost as though floating. I never really noticed that on the way here but then I can't say I remember seeing legs moving under that black gown. Being lost somewhere like this was a daunting idea—it was literally in the middle of nowhere—but the pathos kept getting further away and I think I was starting to panic. I remember seeing his slight and dark outline move upwards over what looked like a high gravelled dune and I just knew that once I had lost sight of him he would be gone. It seemed a long enough struggle just to arrive at that dune and climbing it seemed unreasonable. I really expected him to poke his head over that ridge above me just to see where I was, but I feared he had lost me deliberately. I remember looking around in all directions for a short-cut or familiar ground but there was nothing, just endless rocks and that horizon of purple sky. For the first time, I was feeling the effects of the terrain, I felt blistered, tired and my mouth was dry. I desperately tried to call out for someone but no words came out. The panic had escalated and my need felt so great that something had to give. That was it, the last I remembered of the scene.

My next conscious memory was one of the following mornings around that particular time (1991-92) being aware that something strange had taken place and left its mark on me. I seem to remember dismissing it as another of those dreams where, upon waking, I was left with its evidence. I only had recall of the dream through the sensation of pain, as though I had been on a rigorous hiking trip. There were blisters on my feet and sores all over my hands where I remember having clambered over rocks for something. Even though I insisted this was only a dream, my wounds seemed to hurt more when I recalled the moments that caused them I remember looking up the word psychosomatic and going to libraries to find out what the effects of this condition were. I had been hoping to find something on dreams and whether they could actually leave their mark the same way that physical complaints are said to be caused simply through a frame of mind. I found nothing that would explain my mystery and it was unnerving how I didn't even consider UFOlogy or the paranormal given that it was a subject of interest.

I remembered going away thinking my problems might have been psychosomatic and that these sensations could have been caused by thought, although it was funny how the supernatural never even entered the equation.

All of these new memories pointed to so many strange occurrences throughout my life and I was beginning to see patterns and references. The newly recalled "batch of scenes" took place around a time of my life that was psychologically cloaked, causing me to accept things like they were supposed to happen. The scenes would explain that strange addition to my theatrical interest at the time, "pathos", and why it held such mysticism.

As I sat and carefully pondered over these times so many lifelong fixations returned offering an explanation. That cartoon I once saw as a child of the Charles Dickens play A Christmas Carol where shrouded beings led Scrooge on an abstract journey, one which included the future, started to make sense. I honestly felt I was being shown the future with a pathos mime leading me there. There is something about abstract journeys and their silent (telepathic?) guides and so many other things I describe that tell a hazy but quite legitimate story. For most of my life I had been on journeys and experiences that perhaps only folklore could explain.

The journeys themselves are quite typical of something already known by the descendents of ancient tribes who try to carry on their traditions and folklore. The Shamans or tribal medicine men of northern Asia, who claim to be able to control spirits good and evil, are said to go on such a journey to find a cure for the sick and dying. The journey experienced has often been dismissed as the delirium of those in a sick state which we all suffer at times, but there is still so much to be said for the legitimate spiritual side of the journey. Many come back to report both accurate and identical experiences, some of being led somewhere by a mystical being. I was neither sick nor dying but I seriously believe that the pathos leading me was definitely trying to teach or convey something in the usual psycho-dramatic, alien way. I began to grasp parts of the lessons. The lessons had taken place towards the end of '91 yet I wasn't allowed to remember them until today, 10 years later. Perhaps I reached the maturity to understand them better and maybe 10 years from now I will have the full picture.

The recent revelations I believe taught me something about omnipotence and how to multi-exist. Maybe the first scene of the futuristic street with its multi-faceted business showed me how to exist in the future and provided glimpses of what it might hold such as floatadromes and the new ways of mining whereas the apparitions were an actual test on mastering the presence. I didn't feel like a ghost and simply couldn't do it so maybe that became shelved for another day? My other experiences of the civilised apes and the otherworldly Hindu garden were also hints of a much greater world somewhere that I will only be able to explore fully when I am truly capable.

The new revelations were staggering especially as I thought I had just finished a book about the experience and I wasted no time at all in feverishly jotting down everything I could remember. Whereas I had previously completed a book left with a question mark, I found that recent developments had finally attempted to answer something. The absurdity of the phenomena, an aspect that had plagued me due to its disparity and embarrassment was suddenly starting to speak volumes. Maybe it wasn't so absurd now that I could think of it in terms of psycho-drama and the significance behind its vague symbolism. The pathos tried to convey something perhaps because I desired it so much. It was a case now of going home and adding this essential afterthought to a mostly unsolved volume of secret memoir. I couldn't help wondering whether the forces-that-be had deliberately spared this recent chunk of knowledge as something to consider for the rest of my life.

So where was any of this supposed to leave me? I feel afraid to put this full stop on the saga in the event that even more buried memories suddenly show up and throw everything I have understood into disarray. Sometime that emergence will be inevitable but I hope the next phase will be much further down the line. There have been periods where nothing has happened for years and I am left feeling that all the information I have is the total recall but there would be no sense in that; it's like telling somebody half a story. More will emerge and any new memories I receive from now on will be compiled for a second book of my saga, if there ever is a second book.

I have no interest in trying to extract more half-baked information from myself only to encourage the sceptic's view that it is actually irrational or misinterpreted. It is too easy to extract and taint insufficient knowledge this way when it simply isn't ready. Memories choose to leak at inappropriate times and those times have proved to lack any sort of pattern other than being activated by something but at least now I will be prepared for that. Only once I believed I activated something deliberately by going to sleep one night and requesting it, something which seems to work, but I won't be trying that again out of fear, fear of what I might actually get from that abyss. There isn't anything now that I particularly want to trigger as I am still in the process of making head and tail of what I've already been given.

To be honest, my energy levels are left shatteringly low and I would much rather get on with my life now and enjoy the anonymity I have insisted upon, counting my blessings that I have not been devastated by these encounters. That may be a rarity for someone plunged unwillingly into unexplored paranormal territory, but then my feelings of drainage have proved to be the drawback. Para-psychological interaction with its mind control and disruptive revelation seems to have taken its toll on my actual life-force because I believe that is where the interaction takes place. It has taken a great deal out of me and quite often I feel particularly shell-like as though a spiritual vacuum has been somehow operated.

It was very pleasing that these new revelations did take place offering this hope against a backdrop that seemed quite incomprehensible but perhaps the drainage I feel is the price paid for that hope. It seems I have paid for new information. My new insight will keep me going and on a confident quest for answers instead of psychiatry.

I have requested help along the way without going into any detail of why my mind and energy has been sapped like it has. My recent holiday abroad helped me to recoup on a certain level but I feel the effects of this unknown interaction go untraceably deep. I remember reading Karla Turner's Into the Fringe, a story about alien abduction, in which she learned that towards the end of her episode, alien beings were implanting and extracting information from her actual aura. This was interesting because I often felt that data was somehow seeded and harvested in me on a level that wasn't really mental or physical. I felt that energy was being manipulated at all times and when information was released into my consciousness it followed with a drawn, taxed feeling. Psychic healers are said to work with energy fields and often diagnose so many of our complaints as being a disparity in our fields. Like everything, I prefer to think of this energy as something that can one day be put under the microscope and manipulated the way that aliens obviously can. At the moment it isn't anything I could ever bring to the doctors I've seen or even suggest as a culprit of my condition, but owing to the recent considerations I have made along with the comments in Dr Karla Turner's book, something is at last getting explained

Since I had been advised unfit for work and passed from doctor to doctor in a vain attempt to understand what was actually wrong with me, there have been some rough diagnoses. I have been suspected of suffering from some sort of chronic fatigue illness, while others considered me to have had a nervous stroke because of hyperactivity. I have always felt there was this abundance of nervous energy in me that seems to cause conflicting feelings of lethargy and restlessness. One doctor had thought this might be related to a dysfunctional lobe on the brain similar to the symptom that causes epilepsy and referred me to a hospital for a computerized tomography (CT) scan to monitor the brain's neurological activity. The outcome of this scan was particularly interesting as it showed an unusual amount of electricity in me and one of the doctors had asked if I experienced static at times. I said that I did and went on to ask what the excess electricity actually meant but she seemed to shrug it off as unimportant.

I never did learn what the connection was to a person's electricity and the other neurological symptoms let alone the alien interaction, but I understood that neurotransmitters in the brain use electrical currents. I have had so many incidents where I have affected electrical equipment around me and it has never really been addressed like all my other unexplained symptoms. Different neurological disorders are diagnosed everywhere in the world, but it isn't often that the depth of these disorders are truly explored. What exactly is it that psychics home in on when they discover disparities in energy? Could this be the electricity behind the chemical reactions recognised by doctors or maybe the essential life-force we possess?

When you have come to accept the existence of alien entities and the truth about their involvement in your life, the symptoms left by their interference becomes secondary. I can handle the toll of hyperactivity, excess nervous energy and the drainage and even the incredible effects of static interference, but I would like to know the science behind it all and why alien interaction does this. One essential component for my writing is to share these experiences and learn whether or not I am not alone with their effects.

I also wonder if cases of demonic possession ever leave this aftermath on a person and what a foreign spirit inhabiting somebody actually means for them when the spirit departs. I feel I have been possessed by foreign entities for most of my life. All of them seem to have departed forever. They have caused me to be isolated, allowed me to be smart and left me like an empty shell when their presence finally left.

My neurology and physiology remains very strange through their interaction and there are times when I struggle to contain myself. My entire Neuro Linguistic Programming (NLP) and movement have always been sudden and intense, something which occasionally scares off animals and I also suspect that people notice these movements as though they were the mannerisms of a junkie. I am also extremely sensitive to the environment around me and suffer a particularly low tolerance to any sort of discomfort. This means I find myself ruling out a number of everyday things that might violently disagree with me.

The excess nervous energy I suffer from feels so much like the recognised excess of electricity and often it feels as though I am restraining turbulent currents. Owing to the heightened sensitivity I feel, I have great difficulty in keeping still and sleeping has always been a problem. I seem to display all the movements of somebody with a nervous disposition and the doctors I've seen probably haven't ruled out the possibility of Tourette's Syndrome.

Apart from the telekinetic effects I sometimes have on radios and television, there isn't anything I suffer with that can realistically be attributed to alien intervention. There is the other aspect of my neuro-physiology that I have been reluctant to label as either psychosomatic or paranormal as it seems a bit of both. The physical effects I experience after an incident I believe to have been psychological can be very interesting because my mind seems to have generated them. After awakening from those interactive dreams, would find physical marks as if they actually took place. More interesting is the way I experience these marks even when trying to recollect the incidents. After that vivid spell I had after seeing a perfectly normal mime act in the street, I actually remembered feeling some of the sore and exhaustive effects of frantically following the creature home that time. I became gaspingly thirsty from the desert air I experienced ten years beforehand and my kneecaps suddenly hurt. Feeling the same fear when re-living an episode is quite normal but the physical effects are something quite unusual. Had there been an x-ray at hand when I relived this episode would it have picked up the wear and tear of my soreness like in the effects of stigmata?

I was left with the usual questions that perhaps could never be answered, but I learned profound lessons about my experiences. I felt that all of this might have been a preliminary for the rest of my life. The time up until 1996 seemed to have been a schooling period and then upon my graduation I began a period of learning, about myself and the universe.

My conclusion about what it all meant had to be left open but what occurred to me about the interactors of my life was that they were not just inhabitants of the physical universe or an inter-dimensional realm but might possess the omnipotence of both. That ultimate question about whether they were from outer or inner space could be answered by a possibility that they exist on other planets as well as other planes of reality. They might have even originated from the aforementioned planet but evolved enough onto a level of a "paradigm shift," something we hear a lot of in metaphysics and new age study that, it is believed, one day will transform humans spiritually.

The omnipotence lesson seemed to have been the most significant and I'm not sure what that will mean for the human race or me in years to come. I have been provided the insight to experience multi-perception, multi-consciousness and maybe even glimpses of the future, but none of this has appointed me to a specific role. I would like to consider myself a seer with the gift of saving others from tragedy but like the very few people in the world today who have this gift, I am powerless to switch it on and off at will. Even our most respected psychics who claim mastery of their gift aren't always able to make full use of it when needed. Instead, a manifestation of oddities will occur when the consciousness dwindles, like dropping off to sleep.

Psychic interaction can be terribly one-way and always in the interests of those on the other side, the ones who ultimately call the shots. Our wavelengths are confusingly different and only when we learn to master the science behind that difference will the veil between the living and the dead, the terrestrial and extraterrestrial, the psychic and the physical be lifted forever. Those we regard as our gifted clairvoyants will at last use the potential of their powers and those who have glimpsed or had some level of exposure to the "otherness" as I have will be granted the answers they deserve. My claims and theories can only gather substantiality once the larger picture reveals itself, either from the past or future.

My revelation continues...

Postscript

Glimpses of Tomorrow

As commented earlier, an ongoing memory recall makes finishing a story immensely difficult, as it is a story that develops continually. I still get memories and partial recalls long after completing the last chapter.

However, it isn't my intention to write another chapter about more disjointed tales of improvable interactive experiences. This small section I want to add here is not about me but something that ultimately involves everyone and something that everyone wishes to know about—tomorrow. Amongst the strange scenarios that I have experienced throughout my life, many of them, including new ones, have allowed insights into a possible future existence. We normally call these experiences premonitions, but in my case, they have been hazy scenarios that I have inadvertently plunged into and experienced first hand.

Premonitions do not always warn of impending disaster such as plane crashes or tragedy. Sometimes they can be quite trivial and seemingly irrelevant. If they do manage to steer us away from unpleasant outcomes, it would suggest that a greater godlike intelligence was delivering them and disaster would never strike. I believe that there are genuine seers in the world, governed by such a benevolent force but they are few and far between, with limited powers. In my case, I have been blessed with enough psychic privilege to accidentally gain glimpses of what will be. These glimpses are neither granted nor selected and don't appear to be connected with me in any way. They don't seem to be of any great significance to mankind either but in the words of Roy Walker, I just *"say what I see."*

What you are about to read in this small supplement is not at all subjective nor a guaranteed account of the future written in stone. It is my personal attempt to mix and match all that I have come across to present a rough guide to what the future might hold. Snippets of insight and information can paint a confusing picture, but I hope that there are people out there perceptive enough to help address what I have seen. As with my experiences and my book, it is as much of a quest for answers as it is to provide them.

These are just some of those obscure glimpses alongside my interpretations:

Eclipse: A simple game of the future?

Recently, I believe I had the experience of seeing and partaking in some sort of future video game requiring no screen or joysticks. The action seemed to by psychically controlled and displayed as a type of hologram.

What I remembered seeing were two disks that each player controlled, a light one and a dark one, and the purpose was quite simply for one disk to eclipse the other. It may sound dull and perhaps easy but I was amazed how engaging it actually became! To completely smother a moving object that is trying to smother you is harder than it looks. I believe that the play area or screen became smaller as we played, adding challenge to the game. Points were scored with each total eclipse of the other.

I cannot remember who I played against or even how well I did, where and why it took place or when. Eclipse was a name I coined after I had a gist of how the game was played. The word eclipse seemed the most fitting.

When you consider how involved video games have become these days, and how unfathomable they are to adults, perhaps in the future we return to the simple and minimalist games like Pac Man or Space Invaders. Apart from the psychic and holographic aspects of this strange game, it would not be difficult to manufacture and I welcome anyone to patent it. Like a simple game of marbles, it sounds banal but is a surprisingly engaging way for the tomorrow people to amuse themselves.

Virtual time travel theme parks

There were certain phenomena I came across during my interactive experiences that gave way to the notion of "dual-presence" and psycho-dramatic play scenes. Quite often I was plunged amongst the most lifelike scenes that weren't quite real upon closer inspection. I wasn't actually where I thought I was. These scenes were perhaps the most convincing virtual reality we could achieve without headsets yet the experiencer could still see the real environment if they chose to. In the past I have had these scenes induced into my mind in order to convey important messages by the alien beings as demonstration. It is no doubt a communicative method of the future.

My premonitions seemed to have concentrated a great deal on strange exhibitions or theme parks of either the future or elsewhere. So many times I experienced dreamlike scenarios of specially sectioned areas devoted to a time, a place or a particular theme. Theme parks or reserved areas for special interest have great significance in the future and are a major part of research and entertainment. In the nearer future, they are not necessarily the holographic or induced virtual reality that I have had but rather a physical part of our lifestyle. Much, much later when their interest picks up, they are to become similar to what I describe above. There will be a time when you can visit a theme park that features a particular decade and step right into a virtual reality scene of yesteryear. It is a recording or a playback of time as it actually was. This is achieved through the same principle of traditional ghostly sightings which parapsychologists believe to be playbacks of actual events rather than spirits of the dead. We will reach a time where we discover what ghosts actually are and manage to exploit them. Tomorrow we appear to discover time travel but not the way we thought, not physical time travel. We will manage to create holographic videos of what was and walk among them like they were phantom worlds.

What better way to learn about history? Time travel without interfering with the past. But then do we? Like many, I wonder if the UFOs we see today are those from the future jumping into similar theme parks. It would explain so much about the renowned alien evasiveness.

I recently recalled a dream about being in a place similar to Disney World and visiting exhibitions featuring the history of each country. Some of the histories didn't seem quite correct as though things took place that weren't correctly recorded; this would stand to reason. History books haven't always been accurate. When I visited the theme of my own country, for instance, I was taken back to a scene of Victorian London—horses and carts, harsh looking architecture, and everyone dressed in the drab clothing of the day, yet right in the middle of the scene was a type of fete. There were often village fetes in those days, but what I remembered seeing was an elaborate and technical carousel that could not have been built then. It was the centre of attraction and resembled a landed spacecraft more than a fairground attraction, something the history books could not have chronicled. As always, my memory of the event was as vague as it was limited but it made me wonder if much of the world's true history has been shrouded or if the universe has perhaps a range of parallel pasts, the aforementioned could have been existence. There have been many events in my life of high strangeness that sometimes points to the could have been realm.

Holographic communications

The virtual reality theme parks are not the only holographic sensation in the future. I have seen remarkable displays of apparitions where people can contact each other this way just like a 3D "see-you-see-me" function. It is very similar to the Star Wars film where a recorded hologram of Princess Leah was beamed from R2D2 in order to convey an urgent message. This is even better because the image can be live and materialise from thin air. I have seen this done during interactive experiences of events I believe to have been the future, one of them being aboard an old fashioned train. The apparitions seemed to have become so familiar that a ghost zapping out nowhere is commonplace.

Tomorrow, they seem able to manipulate light so it is without source, shape it, mould it and alter its reflection in order to achieve perfect holograms or even invisibility.

I also get the impression that a phenomenon like telepathy or remote viewing is used because the apparition is aware of the environment. Perhaps the people of tomorrow can project themselves this way, the way we send live transmissions. Perhaps I have materialised like this on many occasions and been mistaken for a ghost.

Ape-schooling and a future "Ganges"

One of the most prominent and recurring memories I have in terms of experiences are of a strange place that resembles the banks of the holy river Ganges. Around this area, strange blue people resembling Hindus bathe by a sacred river while highly evolved seals and apes freely interact. I cannot be certain if this is on another planet or somewhere in the future, but the only thing we know of, pointing to this, is perhaps the Hindu heaven— Nirvana. Hindu art does often feature such a place in their paintings where noble bluish beings reside by lakes in a type of paradise.

The thing that strikes me most is that it is always the same place, a highly familiar location with recognisable features. I am taken there during the Oz Factor and witness magic among ongoing tasks that we as humans are not familiar with. Alien creatures resembling seals with great wisdom rest along the banks with the also-wise blue people. Nearby, there is a race of man-beasts who wander freely and live in the forests. They are not savages but intelligent, talking apes which I suspect are newly evolved from monkeys and being schooled in some way.

I once thought of the river, the Hindus, the seals and the apes of being separate experiences, but now I realise they are all part of the same place. This is a particular area of great wisdom and benevolence, an actual location that humans don't know about. Its familiarity screams at me at times and there are moments when I almost realise where and what it is. Sadly that is it. The déjà vu sensation is rudely snatched away and I am left confused and in the dark again. I will get to know that Nirvana place one day.

The future of aeronautics

It probably comes as no surprise that aircraft develops rapidly in the future because it is that way now. The opinion I had of future aircraft is that they get bigger, much bigger. I previously commented on seeing twin-bodied airliners in the sky, but since then it became even more fabulous. Between huge wings, I have seen triple bodies, even additional wings where the craft was both longer and much wider. With such a gigantic aircraft with its relative weight and passengers, you would expect an earth-thundering roar of engines, but they are much quieter than our own. I don't remember seeing any propulsion. During the times where I have witnessed UFOs, they were immensely large without any sound or signs of propulsion. Maybe we soon learn a profound lesson from the space man's craft and their technology.

In addition to the size of these new planes and the technology, I have witnessed miraculous rescue operations of other aircraft. On one occasion I witnessed (from a TV screen during a strange documentary) a smaller aeroplane in trouble and a larger one coming to its rescue. The periled aeroplane, similar to our own in size was shooting upwards leaving a trail of black smoke behind when a much larger craft swooped above it with astounding speed and latched on to its roof magnetically with a type of suction device below. The older and smaller plane with its doomed engines was carried off to safety. I guessed that passenger craft of the future have ways to detect if another plane is in trouble and have the means to rescue it if needed.

Apart from the magnetic suction device which I think is already used in military aircraft, there is nothing we send into the sky that can manoeuvre that way. The larger craft demonstrated fantastic speed without any acceleration rate as though it swerved upon a magnetic field. Now there's a thought.

Going inside the future city

There was a fantastic experience I commented on earlier that displayed the credentials of both science and high strangeness. I found myself in what seemed the globe-like cabin of a spacecraft descending into a futuristic city. The buildings were awe-inspiring and commercially gigantic where I actually saw the McDonald's food chain take up an entire boulevard. There was more to this story than I struggled to remember. Since then, some of it has crystallised with intriguing revelations.

I had the ability to project from that craft into any of the buildings below. It is unclear how I chose which one but I immediately found myself inside without any knowledge of the transition. My surroundings were a type of living quarters inhabited by people who obviously didn't know I was there. I would have described my entrance as dramatic, similar to a sudden rush of wind, but I seemed to be the only one aware of this. As far as this scenario went, I was a phantom inside a strange futuristic home.

It was a living quarters, with a very pleasant ambiance and a soft light that came from nowhere—a phenomenon I no longer wondered about. The people inside seemed strange; they walked about completely naked showing an unusually pale skin with striking ginger-red hair. I counted about five, male and female, possibly a family. They appeared to be acting no differently to the way any family would act at home, only without clothes. Perhaps I wasn't there long enough to make entire sense of the scenario or get a gist of what engaged them (no signs of dining, TV, computers, etc.) but I remembered hearing in the background the most unusual and beautiful music. I couldn't find the source. From all around came this catchy tune that I couldn't mimic, no vocals, just instruments that sound nothing like any of the synthesisers we have today.

That was all my memory would allow of this scene. What I witnessed was perhaps a striking glimpse of the tomorrow people, either alien hybrids or simply a new generation looking and acting quite differently. The only things convincing me that this wasn't an alien planet were the hallmarks of modern Earth life that I recognised such as the McDonald's logo. That one trademark was perhaps the most absurd yet memorable part of the trip making me realise that this was definitely Earth of tomorrow.

Future incarnation in UFO event

Reincarnation is one aspect of the paranormal that I have not considered enough although I believe that many times I have experienced events from the perspective of others. This particular experience led me to the belief not of a past live but perhaps a future one:

My memory (as often) brought me into the middle of a scene involving hoards of people whom I was trying to conduct and protect. It was night-time at some sort of military base where dozens of uninvited civilians had arrived quite unexpectedly. I was one of a number of military personnel guarding a sealed-off area where an unknown, brightly lit craft had either voluntarily landed or crashed. The scene was pandemonium and I believe we (the military) were alerted at very short notice about this landed craft.

We had expected neither the situation nor these trespassing civilians and I remembered feeling quite embarrassed and defensive about the situation.

Like many scenarios of this nature, the before and after was absent, so I can only guess what this was about, even though it seemed obvious. It was one of those security alerts involving a crashed craft like the famous Roswell incident where the military were called out to intervene and deny the incident to witnesses. I was a soldier of the future or even of the past who had the job of being the bad guy, silencing or lying to witnesses. I remembered feeling angry about their trespassing and interference knowing that I could not deny the glaring and obvious alien craft behind me. It was a futile task but I knew full well there were higher brass I had to report to who would certainly reprimand us all if a successful smokescreen was not delivered.

Who on earth was I, or more importantly, when was I? I briefly remembered one of the other officers addressing me as Carl and my physical appearance was quite different. I was tall and dark-haired, with a moustache, dressed in what seemed to be a blue uniform like the Royal Air force. Interestingly, the landed craft that I tried to keep secret from the public, I seemed to know something about and I didn't find myself awestruck by its presence. This alone points to something of tomorrow because today's military are not that familiar with these things. At least not that we know of.

The brightness of the craft made it incredibly difficult to conceal, turning night almost into daylight. It resembled a dome with brighter flashes of light emitting periodically from its body. Looking at it would have been harsh on the eyes but my job was to keep the civilian crowd in order and I seemed to know what it was. This is fascinating.

Either a parallel life, a future incarnation, or a memory of a past life, I could not say. Whatever or whenever, it still seems that the military will be at the cutting edge of UFOs and their technology.

The influence of Masonry revealed

Throughout Earth's history, secret covens and Masonic bodies have had a great deal to do with religion and society's development. Ancient Egypt, the Knight's Templar and the Dead Sea Scrolls have had important parts to play in the world's history yet have been shrouded from day one. I believe this changes in the future.

The more we truly learn about the occult the less secret these societies will become. There will come a day where the sacred powers that Masons are involved with will be shared with those responsible enough. The Masonic lifestyles will become the norm because society gravitates that way.

Hindus and Buddhists play an enormous part in popular religion and branch out onto Christianity. Some religions will even merge. I have also seen the choice of daily dress involving robes and saris, albeit futuristic ones.

The following snippets of information are partly new and partly to do with previous experiences from earlier chapters. What I find interesting is that there seems to be a consistency regarding places and themes. They reoccur a number of times, and I feel this speaks volumes about premonitions and the future:

Mountainous planet with purple sky

There is a strange but familiar location I have visited on more than one occasion of a heavy dry atmosphere, endless rocky terrain and an unforgettable deep purple sky. It is safe to say that this could be another planet because there is nowhere on Earth quite like it. However, we could be looking at a post-apocalyptic Earth with an ecosystem so badly damaged that even the sky changes colour?

Photographic stills…of moving images

The handheld photographs (stills) of tomorrow are no longer still. I have seen, similar to classic films about magic or fairytales, 3D moving images within the flat photograph. There are some very huge leaps with photography in the future involving holograms and 3D cameras.

Telepathy and better understanding

Telepathy will be commonplace in the future, so that emotions and meanings can become properly conveyed rather than misinterpreted. From my experiences, I have come to the conclusion that all disputes and disagreements are the result of misread signals and meanings. Telepathy is the ultimate in understanding. It transcends all languages and expressions and nobody is ever asked to repeat themselves. Messages can be delivered through oral-telepathy (voices in the head) or impression alone.

When we properly acquire this gift, I doubt there will be any more mysteries to discover.

Flotation in air

There will come a time where we overcome gravity and make the natural forces work with us instead of against us. I have seen airborne flotation used for both industry and leisure.

Strange hybrid cattle

In the strange realm I termed Nirvana, with the sacred river and mysterious blue beings, I believe there are some sort of cattle. I have seen non-descript animals grazing in huge fields that are neither from our world or our time. They resemble a type of mammoth, only much larger with an ill-proportioned head. Their bodies are nearly three times the size of an average elephant, yet their heads resemble a camel's and are only slightly larger. All of them have the same brown fur and appear to be docile grass-eaters there to be farmed. If this is the future and is related to Hindus, I would be surprised if these animals are bred to be eaten.

No doubt there is a farming master plan of which I have
only seen a fragment.

To date, this is the extent that my memory will allow for the above premonitions. Like any other hidden memories, further premonitions will surface in their own good time. I dare say there are more memories of tomorrow that will annoyingly reveal themselves while this page is still warm off the printer. I can only hope that the new batch of forecasts will be relevant, revelations of coming disasters that I could perhaps help avert. But then, I do not choose, I only experience.

I believe that when we experience premonitions, they are only possible future scenarios and not the un-bendable definite fate of tomorrow. Reality's timeline is littered with possibilities and could-have-been scenarios (parallel realities) from which we steer, both good and bad. In other words, we all live through the luckily avoided tragedies which we take for granted as well as missed opportunities. Premonition can be a fantastic tool if it helps us to recognise both possibilities and warnings.

Only time will tell.

About the Author

Now at the age of 36, there is little to be said about the author or his life as he has lead what would appear to be an unfulfilled existence lacking in the achievements and developments most of us go through.

On the other hand there is this life.

1) Despite a life-long interest in the paranormal, the author was convinced that his strange preoccupation only happened to those in high places and not his own mundane existence. What he did not realize was that this 'programmed' idea also came from above.

2) The Otherness was not just about another side of the reality we know but the hidden other life of the author himself. So much goes on in the realm of dreams and the subconscious that maybe we all lead a double life. The author walked right into his!

3) The author wanted to tell a story of friendly Martians coming to save us but nothing is ever that simple. Interaction is a complex but marvelous thing which demonstrates through the use of bizarre mind games that masonry, ancient folklore and the paranormal are all quiescently linked.